THE INTELLIGENT CHIROPRACTOR'S GUIDE TO SURVIVAL

Your Manual for Navigating Personal Injury in an Ethical and Profitable Way

WITH FOREWORDS BY DR. CARL S. CLEVELAND III AND BILLING EXPERT SAM COLLINS

SHAWN STEEL, ESQ. & ALEXANDER C. EISNER, ESQ.

Jacobs & Whitehall
73-03 Bell Blvd, #10
Oakland Gardens, NY 11364
(888) 570-7338
www.jacobsandwhitehall.com

Ordering Information:

Quantity sales. Special discounts are available on quantity purchases by corporations, associations, and others. For details, contact the publisher at the address above.

Orders by U.S. trade bookstores and wholesalers. Please contact Jacobs & Whitehall: Tel: (888) 991-2766 or visit www.jacobsandwhitehall.com.

Printed in the United States of America

Published in 2022

ISBN: 978-1-954506-15-2

DISCLAIMER

This publication is intended to be used for educational purposes only. No legal advice is being given, and no attorney–client relationship is intended to be created by reading this material. The authors assume no liability for any errors or omissions, or for how this book or its contents are used or interpreted, or for any consequences resulting directly or indirectly from the use of this book. For legal or any other advice, please consult an experienced attorney or an appropriate expert who is aware of the specific facts of your case and knowledgeable about the law in your jurisdiction.

Shawn Steel Law Firm

3010 Old Ranch Parkway, Suite 260
Seal Beach, California 90740
(949) 551-9000
www.shawnsteel.com

For Cheyenne and Siobhan—SS

For Grey and Elliott—ACE

TABLE OF CONTENTS

FOREWORD BY CARL S. CLEVELAND III, D.C.

For twenty years, Shawn Steel taught ethics and jurisprudence at Cleveland Chiropractic College in Los Angeles. His early morning classes were memorable for young senior interns. Even today I hear from former students that Steel's class helped prepare them for the "real world" and armed them with practical skills for the business of chiropractic.

Shawn's seminars for practicing chiropractors are well attended by graduates across the profession, and they have come to appreciate Shawn's spirited delivery and quality of content. However, Shawn's brand, entertaining as it is, is not what drives chiropractors by the thousands to his seminars. It is his obvious devotion to the profession of chiropractic instilled in him by his mother, a chiropractor who specialized in delivering babies.

Personal injury has had a sordid past in our profession. Today, many people see a Doctor of Chiropractic as a first choice of provider following a motor vehicle accident or workplace- or sports-related injury, but the management of the insurance and legal aspects of personal injury cases still sparks uncertainty and apprehension in many practitioners. I frequently hear experienced doctors say they no longer take personal injury cases because they do not wish to deal with personal injury attorneys. Enter this book, *The Intelligent Chiropractor's Guide to Survival*.

The release of this book could not be more timely, and the need has never been clearer. For the Doctor of Chiropractic who masters the skills and has the confidence to navigate the essentials of the documentation and legal elements of personal injury trauma case management, the patients are the beneficiaries. Shawn and his partner Alexander Eisner set out to prepare practitioners to do just that and, in my opinion, have achieved their objective.

Today's chiropractors have this invaluable resource at their disposal, and I sincerely invite you to use this book as such—and then pass it on. Knowledge like this is too valuable to keep to oneself.

Carl S. Cleveland III

President, Cleveland University–Kansas City College of Chiropractic and College of Health Sciences.

FOREWORD BY SAM COLLINS

As the coding and billing expert for chiropractic, I have worked with Shawn for over 25 years co-teaching seminars for HJ Ross Company, California Chiropractic Association as well as all Cleveland Chiropractic College, Southern California University of Health Sciences, and Palmer West Chiropractic College. I can attest that Shawn's knowledge of personal injury is so vast he has forgotten more than most will ever know. His steadfastness for the current trends and needs is never stagnated and has evolved with the industry.

Personal injury claims for chiropractic providers have been a large inroad for chiropractic providers since the 1960s with large growth and acceptance in the 1970s and 80s that is now one of the most sought-after types of care associated with personal injury claims. The acceptance of chiropractic in the personal injury arena has always been a shining light for the profession but with broad access comes challenges.

Shawn Steel has made understanding the management and nuances of personal injury accessible to chiropractors. Coming from a chiropractic family, Shawn has an affinity for the profession and has been a stalwart protector to assure chiropractic providers are treated fairly and fit in their rightful place in the health care system.

Shawn provides accessible and practical protocols to assure providers have the understanding and resources to manage claims properly. His tools to evaluate a personal injury claim are invaluable as not all claims are the same. He has always promoted the ethics in personal injury to assure providers will be paid what is fair and reasonable for providing their patients the best possible care to restore their health.

His teaching style and energy are one that only Hollywood could duplicate. The information is practical, accessible, to the point, and ready to use.

This publication represents decades of experience and knowledge and will be a valuable tool for any practitioner, whether new or seasoned. The step-by-step approach and evaluation tools will assure that, beyond your good care, your claims will be paid and afford your patients their rightful and fair settlement.

PREFACE

This book embodies decades of wisdom amassed over thousands of hours of teaching chiropractors in classes and seminars, handling tens of thousands of personal injury cases, participating in hundreds of thousands of fights with incompetent adjusters, traveling millions of miles around California, and recovering hundreds of millions of dollars for clients ... but that's not why you're reading this. You're here because Shawn Steel's plucky brand can make even the dullest subjects entertaining and because, as of late, his Abbot-and-Costello–esque banter with his partner Alexander Eisner has brought a new charm to the old task of helping chiropractors navigate the world of personal injury without getting screwed by evil personal injury attorneys. To that end, you will find this book both informative and entertaining. It is designed to be read either cover to cover or as a reference guide with each chapter standing alone. Much like one of Shawn and Alex's in-person seminars, the book is full of interjections, tangents, vaguely related anecdotes, and light-hearted teasing of the kind you have come to expect from the silver-haired Bonnie and the millennial Clyde. It is also designed to be timeless. We like to imagine that a dog-eared copy will be passed from doc to doc, furthering the cause of chiropractic empowerment for generations to come. But whether you're a veteran of the personal injury game or just starting out, whether you use this book to prop up a coffee table or to revolutionize your practice, it is our sincere hope that you will experience a newfound joy in personal injury practice after reading this book. It is our belief that when done correctly, personal injury is the most rewarding, gratifying, lucrative, and fun discipline a chiropractor can practice. We hope you enjoy reading this book as much as we enjoyed writing it.

Published in 2022 on the 100th anniversary of the Chiropractic Initiatives Act of 1922 that paved the way for chiropractic nationwide.

INTRODUCTION

Why Write This Book And Who Is It For?

Shawn Steel: This book is not for the small percentage of chiropractors who know all about personal injury and already spend a good deal of, if not most of, their time treating personal injury patients and testifying as expert witnesses. A high-volume personal injury chiropractic practice can be a lucrative business, but it comes with its own unique problems (e.g., courting attorneys and referral partners and negotiating chiropractic bills), which are not within the purview of this book.

Rather, this book is for the other ninety percent of chiropractors who do not know all that much about the legal framework as it pertains to chiropractic and would like to diversify their practices. Perhaps they have consulted on a personal injury case once or twice but have never gotten to really know the system in depth or how it works. Or maybe they take a few personal injury cases per year but have never felt particularly comfortable with them.

I have spoken with many of these chiropractors, and some have expressed a sense of befuddlement with the legal process. I use the term *befuddlement* here specifically because there is a real sense that they don't know who to trust, don't know what all the shifting rules are, and might not even know the logistical basics, such as how—or if—they're going to get paid. The experience can be wildly unpredictable, and chiropractors often find themselves being treated unfairly. Some told me they took on one or even a few cases and put in a great deal of time, effort, and energy on them, but they did not always feel fairly compensated or they found the process overly complicated; some found the process so upsetting that they have refused to take any personal injury cases since.

This book is for the chiropractors who simply want to understand how personal injury law and trial proceedings work, as well as the good they can do in a trial context. Chiropractors will learn how to navigate the system and advocate for themselves as contracted professionals. Personal injury cases can be some of the most lucrative and emotionally satisfying, and we teach the fundamental rules to play the game and get paid.

What Should Readers Take Away from This Book?

Shawn Steel: I want chiropractors to come away from this book feeling like it was an easy read that cleared up a lot of misconceptions about the field. They will feel as though they now have access to a concise how-to guide for navigating the personal injury field in a fun, ethical, and profitable way. After reading this, I want chiropractors to move forward in their practices feeling they are capable, have agency, and have the tools to avoid being taken advantage of.

Alexander C. Eisner: Well said, Shawn. In addition, I want chiropractors reading this book to walk away with information they can immediately put to use in their daily practices. I want them to be able to use what they learned to start improving their workflow, make more money, and make their businesses more profitable right away. Other aspects of the book should be more cerebral—a "slow burn," if you will. I want the book to spark ideas that chiropractors can think about over the long term, ideas that will make it easier, more profitable, and more ethically sound for them to incorporate personal injury consultation into their practices.

What Are the Main Things the Authors Want Chiropractors Who Are Just Getting Started to Know About This Book?

Shawn Steel: We teach chiropractors who are new to the personal injury world all the time. In this book (as well as in our classes and our practice generally), we can give new chiropractors all sorts of information on technology and tools, as well as a straightforward explanation of the field as it stands, as well as a clear path forward. They are the easiest students to teach.

It's the more experienced practitioners who have been beaten up relentlessly for twenty years that tend to have the most trouble learning about the field.

Those chiropractors tend to be relatively gun-shy, have a lot of bad associations, and often have a harder time getting the message.

Thankfully, this book is for both types of learners as long as they want to learn about personal injury law.

Alexander C. Eisner: Shawn and I have many years of teaching this stuff under our belts. Though some things have changed in that time, the basics remain the same. Our goal is to synthesize what we know and what we've been teaching into an easily digestible book and then disseminate it to the people who need it. That way, those people can sit and absorb the tips and tricks we've acquired over the years at their own pace.

Many Attorneys Have Tried to Bridge the Gap Between Law and Chiropractic. What Makes the Authors Uniquely Qualified to Bridge This Gap and Provide This Information?

Shawn Steel: I don't know if other attorneys have really attempted to capture the chiropractic

market because their attempts are often superficial. As leading providers of continuing education on personal injury law and chiropractic in California, we frequently host and attend seminars for chiropractors. Occasionally, other attorneys show up, bring attractive people to sit at their table, and say they love chiropractors, all in an attempt to drum up business. Sometimes they have a marketing scheme of giving away something valuable to get chiropractors to engage with them.

In the end though, they are not familiar with the values of chiropractic. They don't know much about the history of the practice or what motivates people who become chiropractors. They don't know what's going on in chiropractic colleges or how the field has changed and matured over the years. They don't know the scientific considerations or studies behind the field.

As a result, these attorneys approach the community from an opportunistic point of view, casting their lines into the lake and hoping for fish. However, to extend the fishing analogy, it's as if they don't know the first thing about fishing beyond buying a rod and reel. I have yet to see any of them achieve success, specifically because they don't really know how to speak the language or discuss the interests of the community. We have found that this type of attorney tends to not last very long in chiropractic circles.

Alexander C. Eisner: I began my practice on the defense side of personal injury and malpractice, mostly working for insurance companies and defending doctors when they were sued for malpractice. These experiences gave me unique insights into the philosophy of defense in personal injury and malpractice cases. I was forced to consider things like billable hours, providing documentation to adjusters to get authority, and finding inconsistences within a Plaintiff's story. With this level of insight applied to the 'other side,' I have been able to guide both my clients and our partner chiropractors through the legal process efficiently.

After I left medical malpractice, I became a trial attorney in civil practice, but I hadn't quite found my niche. At that point, Shawn and I met serendipitously in what I like to think of as a moment of fate. Shawn had put out an ad for a litigation attorney who was looking for a "life-changing opportunity." I would never tell him this, but it turned out that he was right. The opportunity to work with him was life-changing, and we're headed into our fifth year of forging new paths forward.

I meet many personal injury attorneys at conferences, and they often ask me how we get so many case referrals from chiropractors—specifically, how we manage to get enough referrals to sustain a firm. They are always looking for some trick, supersecret, or methodology that will help them break into the field.

The fact is, though, it just comes down to treating our chiropractors well and making sure we get them paid in full and on time. We also give them the tools to advocate for themselves and to bill reasonably in the field, as well as the ability to weed out bad attorneys and cases. We believe in them, they believe in us, and we all believe in our cases and the patients/clients involved. To that end, we make sure that we're easy to work with and honest. We have our chiropractors' backs, so they have no reason to work with anyone else.

This is how we developed our reputation within the California chiropractic community for being the go-to attorneys for personal injury referrals. I know this sounds like one long commercial for our firm, but in reality, it is a preview of the type of relationship that all chiropractors should have with the personal injury attorneys their patients' engage. Ethical personal injury attorneys are out there. Knowing how to work up cases correctly and how to vet attorneys and cases puts chiropractors in the position of both finding the good attorneys *and* demanding to be treated with the respect chiropractors deserve.

CHAPTER 1

THE RELATIONSHIP BETWEEN CHIROPRACTORS AND THEIR PATIENTS

Shawn Steel: The relationship between a chiropractor and a patient is quite unique. Chiropractic as a field has been practiced for over a hundred years, continually fending off attacks from the larger, more established medical community and the ensuing stigma that became attached to the field. Because of these conditions and the embattled mindset that they can create, the relationship between chiropractors and their patients became, and still is, strong and loyal. If people feel they're receiving cost-effective care that helps them get better, they support the profession and the practitioners that provide that care. These intense patient–chiropractor relationships and the patient demand they create have brought chiropractors into the mainstream, despite the continued malignment from some in the medical and legislative communities.

As we said, this progress is relatively recent. Before the late twentieth century, chiropractors set up shop in out-of-the-way locations where they wouldn't be harassed, and patients had to search to find them. However, since the turn of the twenty-first century, the public perception of chiropractors has changed dramatically, and the field's credibility has increased. It cannot be stressed enough that the driving force of this shift is the patients. As mentioned above, chiropractors sometimes get results for patients that other medical professionals have failed to produce. Patients are becoming increasingly hesitant to rush to primary care doctors who are quick to prescribe drugs rather than treat the musculoskeletal causes of pain.

To some degree, the continued existence of chiropractic is proof that it can be effective. Without good outcomes, chiropractic would have disappeared long ago. Instead, millions of people support chiropractic because they (or people they care about) have benefitted from working with chiropractors.

In this sense, chiropractic is uniquely market driven. It isn't government-driven. It isn't driven by major research universities or medical associations. It isn't driven by think tanks or individual intellectuals. Instead, a free-market demand thrives on the relationships fostered between chiropractors and their patients, as well as the results that chiropractic achieves.

CHAPTER 2

WHY PERSONAL INJURY IS DIFFERENT

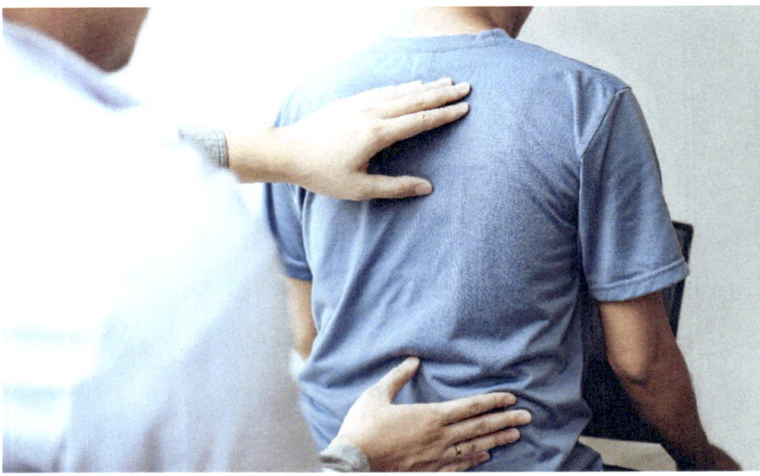

Chiropractors Have a Special Relationship to Trauma That Sets Them Apart from Other Medical Specialists

Shawn Steel: Something that a lot of folks don't realize about chiropractors is that they are trained to deal with trauma. That training is a lifelong, ongoing process. It's an accumulation, rather than something learned all at once.

When most general practitioners and primary care physicians have patients with specific issues that need specific types of treatment and care, they refer those patients to appropriate specialists. For example, if there's a problem with a patient's knee and the patient is seeing a general practitioner or a specialist in a field who can't help the patient (such as neurology), the patient gets referred to a specialist who can help, most likely an orthopedist.

Personal injury trauma is often a whole-body condition that affects multiple body parts with multiple diagnostic problems or injuries. Chiropractors are used to treating patients with many issues present at the same time.

For instance, a chiropractor might treat someone who has low-back problems and arthritic problems and a sports injury such as a sprained knee. When chiropractors first see a trauma patient, all kinds of things may be going on simultaneously. This includes symptoms that may be difficult to pin down at first, situations where chiropractors find out that what they initially thought the problem was, was not, in fact, the problem. In a case like this, a chiropractor may treat a person with a shoulder injury, only to find out a few weeks later that the neck is really the problem. Chiropractors are often well trained for that sort of triage because of their overall musculoskeletal knowledge.

It follows that more people than ever are seeking out chiropractors for traumatic injuries. They also do this because people are simply less interested in drugs and surgery as championed in mainstream medical practice.

Alexander C. Eisner: Many patients are looking for comprehensive, non-invasive, non-narcotic treatment options for traumatic injuries and the resulting pain and mobility issues, and often they are not finding them elsewhere in the medical community. People who go to their primary care physician after an accident are usually given a prescription for some sort of pain pill rather than comprehensive treatment for the underlying problem.

This poses two risks for the average patient: Not solving the underlying problem, and potentially becoming addicted to narcotics.

Amidst the current opioid epidemic, it is incredibly important to have non-invasive, non-narcotic treatment options, and chiropractors have a particularly unique capacity to offer those alternatives.

Chiropractors are also uniquely qualified to serve as quarterbacks or managers of care—keeping track of multiple injuries and multiple therapies to insure that patients get the treatment they need (be it chiropractic or some other specialist care) and that nothing falls through the cracks.

How the Practicing Chiropractor Benefits from Taking on Personal Injury Cases

Shawn Steel: There are a number of ways in which a practicing chiropractor can benefit from taking on personal injury cases.

For one, there is the psychological, moral, and emotional benefit of helping people who are hurting.

These might be people who are badly hurt or have a complicated injury with multiple problems. They might be people who have consulted other medical authorities who have decided against major interventions (e.g., immediate surgery) for them or performed those interventions but they provided little to no improvement.

When successful, chiropractors get the satisfaction of making progress with their patients over the course of their time together and helping them regain their mobility and good quality of life. That kind of sustained progress creates a bond between chiropractors and patients that often lasts a lifetime. This is especially true if the chiropractor was able to offer progress and relief where other medical professionals could not.

I am reminded of a client we had several years ago named Jan. Jan had chronic lower-back pain stemming from a pole-vaulting injury she got in college. After being involved in a moderately serious rear-end collision that exacerbated her pain substantially, she ended up with a chiropractor who referred her to us. She had been taking prescription pain medication for almost a decade after doctors told her there was little else they could do for her back. Having never tried chiropractic before, she was admittedly hesitant to do so, but after the car accident, she was ready to try anything.

Jan recounted, "After ten sessions, I could tell that for the first time, the actual root cause of my condition was being treated, not just covered up. I was so sick of the drugs—and all of the side effects, which just required more drugs—and truly thought my condition was hopeless. At the conclusion of my treatment, I was feeling better than I had felt in a long time, *and* I am no longer taking pain medication."

This is just one of many stories we've heard about a chiropractor establishing a new relationship with a patient and giving the patient confidence that will last a lifetime.

Once established, the relationship between patient and chiropractor may become multi-generational. Parents tend to pass on their confidence in the skills and abilities of a chiropractor to their children. We often see the children of chiropractic patients going to their parents' chiropractor when they start getting into sports in high school or if they start developing any sort of aches and pains or other issues that require a chiropractor's assistance.

These relationships are often the main motivator for chiropractic students. They want to have the satisfaction of being healers, especially across generations. If it were just about money, they could have become stock traders or something exclusively lucrative rather than doing something that actively helps people every day.

However, this doesn't mean that a chiropractor should not make money. In fact, taking on personal injury cases can be financially rewarding. There is a lot of money available for providing effective treatment for trauma patients. Insurance companies take in billions of dollars every year in premiums, and a percentage of those funds is slated to go to providers who take care of trauma victims.

Unfortunately, there are barriers to accessing that money. Insurance companies pay out as little as possible on claims. They are in the business of making and keeping as much money as they can, and they have trial attorneys on retainer to fight nearly every claim. All too often, they attempt to dominate the health care decisions made about patients to avoid making payments. However, chiropractors can become part of a team that helps patients access the funds necessary for their treatment and healing. This can be financially beneficial for the chiropractor, in addition to helping the chiropractor deliver care to patients and the profession as a whole to continue to grow.

So, the bottom line is that the two main reasons for chiropractors to take on personal injury cases are the good they can do for their patients and the compensation they can earn in the process.

Alexander C. Eisner: I would add that many of the chiropractors that I have come to know are dedicated wholly to healing. They are not interested in many of the ancillary considerations or benefits that are common motivators in other specialties. I think that when somebody comes into their office and says, "I've been in an accident and I'm hurting here, here, and here," their instinct to heal kicks in. For them, when they are faced with a personal injury case, simply being a practicing chiropractor who can help is incredibly important and rewarding. It scratches a very specific itch, and it brings home the fact that this is a calling for them.

It should also be mentioned that the profession of chiropractic as a whole benefits any time an individual walks into a chiropractor's office and has a good experience. Any time a patient is healed to any degree by a chiropractor, or given back the ability to do something an injury had taken away, it helps validate the field. Chiropractors believe in their discipline and believe in the power of being able to help patients regain the ability to turn their head left and right or bend over when an accident had left them incapable of doing so. The patient becomes one more advocate walking around in the world attesting that chiropractic is not only real but works and makes life better.

CHAPTER 3

SCREENING NEW PERSONAL INJURY PATIENTS

Shawn Steel: Screening is an absolutely critical first step. When chiropractors meet for the first time with a new patient, they conduct a lengthy examination in accordance with the current guidelines and standards of the American Medical Association. They stipulate that a chiropractor ought to spend a certain amount of time with a patient performing certain diagnostic procedures, depending on the seriousness of the patient's injuries. This is referred to as the initial examination. [1]

Unlike the initial intake examinations in many medical doctors' practices, the chiropractic examination is not conducted by an assistant or a nurse but rather is done by the chiropractor. In addition to fulfilling the standard requirements for intake, the initial examination is an excellent opportunity for bonding between the patient and the chiropractor. Being a great chiropractor involves listening to patients carefully, and a great initial examination involves taking an extensive, detailed medical and injury history. It also involves empathizing with patients and relating to what they're going through.

Most people who are injured and come to a chiropractor have both visible injuries and invisible injuries. Injuries that are invisible, or not immediately visually evident, are associated with a great deal of

[1] We know that many of you know this already. Bear with us. We are starting basic but will quickly get more advanced.

emotional overlay. Often, people with invisible injuries deal with prejudice and a lack of consideration or understanding by society—even by the people closest to them. When people think of injuries, they think of the ones you can see, like a broken arm that requires a cast. When an injury doesn't come with visual clues, some people have a much harder time realizing that someone is hurting. They may not remember—or even believe—that the person is in pain. Consequently, some of these people don't get a lot of sympathy, even from their own families.

Alexander C. Eisner: Insurance adjusters and defense attorneys are all too aware of the fact that so called 'invisible injuries' occur and the ways in which they affect the injured. They routinely exploit this situation at trial by painting those with injuries that lack compelling or obvious objective findings as malingerers or exaggerators, and unfortunately, this tactic successfully exploits the jurors' subconscious bias against invisible injuries more often than not.

Shawn Steel: A good chiropractor will be able to forge a bond with a patient in order to get a true sense of the medical history and the injury and symptoms. Patients will usually be honest with the chiropractor at that point. Out of those honest conversations and physical examinations come diagnoses and treatments.

Of course, there are outliers, especially when it comes to personal injury. There will always be a very small number of patients who grossly exaggerate or lie about an injury and its symptoms. There are a number of reasons people might do this. Some want to get something from their injury (e.g., a diagnosis of a disability, worker's compensation payments, or a personal injury settlement), while others have more complicated emotional needs that they hope to have assuaged by treatment for exaggerated symptoms. All medical practitioners—including medical doctors and chiropractors—are trained to spot obvious fabrications in several ways. In a personal injury context, there are a few tell-tale signs.

For instance, chiropractors watch for a patient's reaction when they suggest a treatment plan that requires relatively little manual manipulation, is easy, and, most importantly, is inexpensive. Most people with severe injuries are thrilled to know there is a simple or cost-effective way to treat their injuries. However, if patients are hoping for a large settlement, they might want a treatment that leads to a large payout.

If there is a relatively simple and cost-effective treatment available, a chiropractor can present it to the patient as such and note the reaction. Some patients might be understandably skeptical that any real solution to their problem would be easy or relatively cheap (especially if they have had bad experiences with other medical professionals). However, if they reject the idea outright and become uninterested once a simpler, more cost-effective treatment is offered, that is something of a red flag (something you should let the Plaintiff's attorney know about right away).

Another way to see if patients are genuinely seeking help is to ask them to pay in cash. This is a less reliable method—as there are a number of reasons people might not be able to pay in cash, especially if they have little income—however, patients who are not genuinely injured will almost never pay in cash. Conversely, the willingness of patients to invest in their own treatment can bolster their cases in the eyes of the ever-skeptical insurance adjuster.

If chiropractors explain that their first priority is the patient's health and that a distant second is the patient's possible financial gain from a personal injury case, this can be incredibly helpful in evoking a patient's true motives. This is not to say that patients looking for an unrealistic payday might not truly be injured. Chiropractors should just make sure in such cases that they are meticulous in their documentation of the medical necessity of treatment and referrals for treatment (they might also consider giving the personal injury attorney a heads up about this situation).

It cannot be stressed enough that chiropractors should avoid bad-faith personal injury cases, including those of people who were in an accident but are knowingly exaggerating the extent of their injuries. There are some chiropractors (and some unethical attorneys) who believe that they can make money by abetting such patients. However, this almost always backfires in the end. These patients are usually quite unreliable and easy for insurance companies to discredit. Insurance companies are likely to determine that accidents involving those types of patients weren't as serious as they are being depicted, and this will result in a minimal to no settlement and a record being made of the chiropractor's involvement.

It also damages one's reputation as a chiropractor. We will discuss reputation more extensively in the ethics section of this book; however, suffice it to say here that a chiropractor only has one reputation. If chiropractors constantly treat people who are grossly exaggerating their symptoms to bolster a weak personal injury case, they start to become associated with that sort of case. The chiropractors' fees and treatments thereafter will only be approved for relatively minor problems, and they may not even wind up getting paid. Certainly, they will not last long in the personal injury community.

The National Insurance Crime Bureau (NICB) closely monitors doctors, attorneys, body shops, and patients for fraudulent activity. They have incredible resources at their disposal to keep everyone in the PI process honest. Make no mistake, if you are reading this book, you almost certainly have a file (or will soon have a file) with the NICB. In other words, your reputation is well documented, so do your best to protect it.

Alexander C. Eisner: Regarding diagnosis, first and most importantly, the chiropractor has to confirm if there is actually something to diagnose. If the patient is describing intermittent pain at level 1 or 2 out of 10, the injury is a low level one that is likely to resolve quickly. This is not the type of injury that results in a diagnosis that makes for a good personal injury case. The patient might be a great one, and the chiropractor may go on to treat the patient in the non–personal-injury part of the practice. However, in terms of a personal injury case, this is probably not where chiropractors want to focus their time and energy.

I point this out because there is a desire, especially when a patient comes in with compelling photographs of a car accident, to see dollar signs and a personal injury workup. Once chiropractors start down that path it can be difficult to change direction, take the hit, and convert the dollar signs to cash payments from the patient. My advice here would be to keep an open mind until all the facts come out. Don't be afraid to admit that the injuries the patient is describing simply don't justify starting a personal injury case in which chiropractic bills need to be paid (Don't forget: That's the goal).

CHAPTER 4

THE IMPORTANCE OF ACCESSING PATIENTS' MEDICAL RECORDS

Shawn Steel: Medical professionals who practice personal injury care should always check to see if there are any relevant medical records. For chiropractors, this includes any records of other doctors who saw the same patient for the same injury (or other injuries that could be considered related prior or subsequent to an accident). Not doing so risks serious malpractice. If there was information in those records that was missed because the chiropractor did not bother to read or even request the records, the chiropractor is much more likely to needlessly fail the patient. In addition to harming the patient and hindering the chiropractor's own ability to provide good practice, this can also open the chiropractor up to malpractice liability.

Chiropractors also need to be able to read these records judiciously. Take, for instance, emergency rooms. Frankly, not all ERs are created equal. Some do complete, thorough examinations and provide well-thought-out treatments, and others are much less thorough, offering more superficial triage reports. The quality and depth of a diagnosis or exam during an ER visit depends essentially on geographic chance. Specifically, it depends on where the person was when they were injured, the quality of the ER, and additional factors such as the date and time in question, how busy the ER was, the individuals who treated the patient (including doctors, nurses, and paramedics), and how cooperative, lucid, and informative the patient was.

So, when chiropractors obtain ER records, they should look carefully at both what was said, what was not said, what was focused on, and what was not focused on. Many times, we see ER personnel performing triage and taking care of aspects of treatment they're most concerned about while ignoring other major injuries because they are not immediately apparent. For instance, we've seen many scenarios where an ER staff is concerned with trauma to the head for the duration of the patient's visit. However, by the time the patient visits the chiropractor, the main concern is something else, such as neck pain. The ER record may have a line that says "patient denies musculoskeletal injury" with a check mark next to it, and an adjuster very well may latch onto this statement in an attempt to discredit orthopedic injuries that are later documented. In this circumstance, it is important to note in the initial chiropractic examination something like, "ER record notes 'no musculoskeletal distress' in ER; however, patient indicates no orthopedic exam was conducted and trauma team was largely concerned with neurologic injuries." This shows that the chiropractor read the record but also smartly corrected the findings at the first available opportunity. Failing to correct this type of error or omission can lead to contradictory records that can become a nightmare in a personal injury case and often lead to the ER doctor *and* the chiropractor having to sit for a deposition to set the record straight.

In other words, chiropractors must educate themselves about the patient's medical records to see if there's something that would or should influence the current diagnosis and treatment plan. Without doing that, chiropractors are flying blind, and this is something they really cannot afford to do when it comes to personal injury trauma.

Alexander C. Eisner: When viewing past medical records, chiropractors should also look for the corroboration and consistency of the patient's accounts of what happened and the current symptoms. In addition, they should look for any information that the patient may have forgotten to mention—or may not have mentioned for whatever reason—when giving accounts and descriptions of the event and the injuries.

Just because patients don't mention something in their initial examination, or in any one of their appointments, doesn't mean they aren't experiencing it. For example, a patient may not be actively complaining of headaches. However, an ER or ambulance record may state that the patient complained of a severe headache in the immediate aftermath of the injury. This could serve as a prompt for the chiropractor to ask the patient about headaches specifically. Notably, this method can be useful whether or not the symptom is still being experienced by the patient. Knowing that there was a headache immediately following an accident can be helpful in forming a diagnosis, even if the headache stopped long ago and never recurred.

As a general rule, chiropractors should remember that every examination and interview of a patient is a snapshot or data point. Just because somebody isn't experiencing pain at the exact moment the person is asked doesn't mean that the person isn't still experiencing that kind of pain intermittently. Therefore, chiropractors need to make sure that they're looking at the records from the ER and the ambulance and any other place where the patient might have reported or displayed relevant symptoms (e.g., police report narratives, fire department or EMT records). They should also look at any treatments that have been tried by previous medical professionals, as well as the patient's reactions and responses to those treatments. This helps the chiropractor to be consistent in following up on all of the patient's injuries and symptoms, rather than the ones the patient happened to mention in the initial examination. As you probably know, patients are not always the best historians of past and present treatments, diagnoses, or causes of injuries. Failing to exercise due diligence to get a good history can leave one with egg on one's face.

CHAPTER 5

WHY (AND HOW) CHIROPRACTORS SHOULD LOOK AT POLICE REPORTS

Alexander C. Eisner: Here are a few practical tips I like to give chiropractors looking to glean information from police reports.

- **P1 is usually the party at fault.** The face sheet or front page of a traffic collision report or police report usually mentions a "P1" or "Party 1," and this is almost always the party that police officers find to be at fault. They usually list the first party as the at-fault party and the second party as the victim. [2]

Shawn Steel: 90% of the time, police reports are mostly accurate.

Alexander C. Eisner: …thanks.

- **The narrative section may provide valuable information on liability.** In these reports, there is often a narrative section toward the end that outlines what happened at the scene according to witness testimony. This narrative can be important for figuring out liability, as well as complaints of injury at the scene. In terms of liability, there will often be a clear indication of which party was at fault (or believed to be at fault) in either witness/party statements or the officer's framing of the situation. In terms of diagnosis, there will often be context clues in the

---

[2] This is not always true, however. In he-said-she-said cases—like red light/green light disputes—where the officers have no idea who to believe, they will randomly assign the parties P1 and P2.

narrative. For instance, the patient may have complained of a head injury or a back injury at the scene, and this can be helpful when assessing current complaints and injuries.

- **Checkbox statements are important.** Somewhere in the middle of the report there is usually a list of prepared statements with checkboxes next to them. The checks indicate whether the police officer suspected alcohol or drugs at the scene, speeding was a cause of an accident, the victim was wearing a seatbelt, and other factors of that nature. The reader can also get a sense of how the officer perceived the patient's affect (e.g., lucid, concussed). This can help inform both treatment and liability.
- **Look for disputed liability.** One thing a chiropractor should look for in a police report is disputed liability, which is indicated by conflicting narratives about what caused the accident (e.g., a statement that both parties claimed to have had the right of way from a green light). The police officer may be unsure

about which party ran a red light and caused the accident. Cases with disputed liability can prove problematic in a personal injury context. Some personal injury attorneys who are especially good at disputed liability cases may be willing to take on the situation and fight it. If that's the case, then the chiropractor is going to want to have an individual conversation with that attorney about the situation before agreeing to take the case on a lien basis, just to make sure that the chiropractor and attorney are on the same page. As a general rule, treating on a lien in a disputed liability case is risky, so chiropractors should do this at their own discretion (more on this later). Remember that chiropractors are not obligated to treat on a lien just because a patient has engaged an attorney. In many cases, chiropractors are the only ones looking out for their own remuneration.

- **Chiropractors have a right to ask questions.** Chiropractors can ask about anything they find in a police or traffic report, including the possibility of disputed liability. If chiropractors believe a case will involve disputed liability and therefore are concerned about the risk, they can and should talk to whichever attorney they're working with about it. It is acceptable not to want to put $4,000 or $5,000 on a lien only to find out a year later that the payment will be, for example, cut in half because the patient was deemed partly at fault.

When there is a concern about who is at fault, attorneys should be able to describe honestly how much risk is involved in putting treatment on a lien. They might be able to offer more information about how the case is bolstered by additional evidence and is, therefore, less of a risk for the chiropractor—or the chiropractor may find that they have no explanation for how they intend to overcome a liability problem and thus ensure the bill is paid.[3]

---

[3] Or they might not be able to get the attorney on the phone at all…a really bad sign.

For instance, an attorney might tell a chiropractor that the case is actually quite sound because an accident reconstructionist has been lined up to testify, footage has been obtained from a red-light camera, or images of the accident are available from a dashboard camera recording of an Uber driver who was in the vicinity of the accident. Or they might look at the evidence and say that the case is actually not great because it's a classic *he-said-she-said* situation, and there's no telling how it might pan out. In any case, the attorney will be aware of the approximate level of risk (barring truly unforeseen circumstances). It should go without saying (but it absolutely doesn't) that the chiropractor should be working with an attorney who will be honest about the risk in taking on the case. The chiropractor should also be examining the primary documents and asking the relevant questions. Remember: chiropractors are the only ones looking out for their own expenses and income, and no one wants to operate a free clinic.

Shawn Steel: That's my line!

How Chiropractors Can Tell if a Patient Is a Good Personal Injury Client or a Risky Lien

Alexander C. Eisner: This assessment comes down to a combination of the things we've already talked about. It's a matter of what the injuries look like, what other records say about the accident (and prior injuries), and how much insurance there is to collect (if any).

There are also several additional factors to look out for that can indicate a risky lien.

- **Damage isn't visible in pictures of the accident.** Ask to see some pictures of the accident, and look for visible signs of damage. It is a bad sign if damage from the accident is not immediately evident in the pictures. After all, if you can't see the damage, the jury won't see it either (Note: I'm being overly simplistic here. There are biomechanics experts and accident reconstruction experts who can explain to juries how to interpret vehicle damage and the forces involved in accidents that may not look particularly bad from the pictures. It is, however, one piece of the puzzle that chiropractors should look out for. Minimal visible damage to a car would be one of the multiple factors that make a case risky to take on lien.).

- **Billboard lawyers have been hired.** You want to be alert to patients who come in with what we call "billboard attorneys." These are attorneys that take most or all of the personal injury cases that come through their doors, regardless of how risky a case might be for a doctor to take on lien. If a patient is being represented by one of these attorneys, it's an indication that the case might be risky (though this isn't always so). As we said, billboard attorneys tend to take all kinds of clients—risky and non-risky—which is why these cases might require a closer look when it comes to risk.
- **Many prior accidents have occurred.** If a patient has had many prior accidents, especially prior accidents with injuries that have been

treated by the chiropractor, things start to look suspicious. If the only complaint is about a body part for which the chiropractor has already been treating the patient and which doesn't appear to be any more injured than it was before the recent accident, that's almost certainly a risky lien. A patient who consults a chiropractor about an injury that has already been treated by many other providers for a personal injury case and who now is seeking treatment from the chiropractor on a lien could also be risky, depending on how much insurance money there is, as well as how large a potential settlement might be (Note: Again I'm being overly simplistic here, but this is another good reason to get a patient's past medical records. Of course, it is possible that a patient is simply unlucky and has had multiple accidents affecting the same body part, but it is unlikely and certainly going to be a red flag to the insurance company.).

There are also clear indications of a *good* personal injury case. They are essentially the opposites of the risky case warning signs. In a good case, **photographs of the accident usually show real damage** that any layperson is able to identify as serious and that could have caused serious injuries. A patient with a good case has **real injuries that have both subjective and objective aspects** (i.e., you can prove that the injuries physically exist and that they are causing real, compelling pain and suffering to the person). Another good indicator is if the person has **plenty of insurance money** available, as this helps ensure payment. While ample insurance money doesn't always indicate a good personal injury case, it does help the chiropractor determine if there is even enough potential money to pay the bill.

Finally, the chiropractor should consider which—if any—attorney a patient is being represented by when the patient seeks out the chiropractor's services. It's a good sign for a personal injury case **if patients come in represented by an attorney that the chiropractor knows to be ethical and responsible.** It can also be a good sign if the patient comes in without legal representation and is willing to go to a personal injury attorney that the chiropractor knows to be ethical and responsible.

Shawn Steel: Typical Alex—takes 700 words to say what I could say in 14. There are four keys to a good PI case: Liability, damages, injury, and insurance.

CHAPTER 6

WHAT CHIROPRACTORS NEED TO KNOW ABOUT ATTORNEYS

Alexander C. Eisner: The relationship between chiropractors and attorneys—especially personal injury attorneys—can be contentious. This is why we strongly suggest working with an explicitly pro-chiropractic personal injury attorney.

It is crucial for chiropractors who want to do personal injury work to find the right attorney or attorneys to work with. Some personal injury attorneys have no idea what chiropractors do, and some think that a chiropractor will be a weak link in the case. Sometimes attorneys are fundamentally anti-chiropractic or even hostile to chiropractors.

Let's say a patient got into a car wreck and decided to see a chiropractor. An anti-chiropractic or chiropractic-hostile attorney may tell the patient to see an orthopedic surgeon first rather than a chiropractor because they believe this will get the patient a larger settlement and increase the perceived severity (and, therefore, the amount of damages) of the personal injury case. The attorney might tell the patient that chiropractors are not very strong witnesses in the courtroom because insurance companies don't like them. Of course, this is not factually accurate, but these sorts of attorneys use old arguments to convince their clients to stop going to their chiropractors. These attorneys probably don't know much about personal injury or the types of trauma people sustain from car accidents. Otherwise, they would know that people that have accidents don't necessarily go to an orthopedic surgeon every single time. There are a number of issues that play out in the body of someone who has sustained a traumatic injury, some of which a chiropractor may be better suited to address than an orthopedic surgeon. In fact, a semi-recent study shows that 29% of people are more likely to see a chiropractor with back and neck pain than even an MD.[4]

If a personal injury attorney doesn't know anything about chiropractic practice (especially when many people that have car accidents see a chiropractor), it tells you that the attorney is probably not well-equipped to competently handle personal injury cases involving car accidents and traumatic injuries. This sort of ill-equipped attorney may consequently be very hostile to the chiropractor and try to steal patients away from a chiropractor they were perfectly happy with. This is what we call the "steal-patient syndrome." Though these attorneys often don't see it coming, such a strong anti-chiropractic approach can work against

---

[4]https://www.palmer.edu/wp-content/uploads/2021/12/gallup-report-palmer-college.pdf

them, especially if their client feels that an ultimatum is developing between the attorney and their chiropractor.

We often get calls about cases like this. Patients complain that they were seeing a chiropractor, but their attorney insisted they stop and go to a medical clinic instead. Patients often say that the medical clinic's approach is too cold and insensitive and that doctors pushed drugs or injections when patients preferred to stick with a more naturalistic approach. In these cases, patients often wind up firing the attorney who told them to quit seeing their chiropractor, and hiring an attorney their chiropractor recommended to them (a pro-chiropractic attorney).

The other thing chiropractors should know about attorneys has to do with their motivation. A plaintiff's personal injury attorney works on a contingency fee basis, meaning the attorney doesn't get paid until and unless the client gets paid and makes a set percentage of that payout. Because of this dynamic, attorneys are always trying to maximize the gross amount recovered for the client. In theory, this is good for everyone. The more money a case settles for, the more money there is to go around. The more money there is to go around, the higher the likelihood that the chiropractor's bill doesn't end up on the chopping block. However, in an attempt to increase case value, attorneys are prone to doing things such as insisting that clients see lots of different doctors and get lots of expensive tests. They do this because, if the policy limit supports it, it is often true that the higher the medical bills the higher a case's settlement value. This, of course, does not always lead to the best outcome for the patient.

Certainly, attorneys' motives are not always misguided, and, of course, some patients actually need referrals to or treatment by physicians in addition to chiropractors. It is, however, important to keep in mind the underlying motivation of most personal injury attorneys. This should allow one to keep an eye on the medical well-being of the patient and not allow a substitution of the attorney's legal judgment for the chiropractor's medical judgment. When things are operating optimally, a personal injury case should be a collaboration among specialists with different perspectives (wherein the attorney is but one) who come together to maximize the patient's fiscal and psychological recovery.

Lastly and maybe most obviously, remember that attorneys are human beings just like chiropractors. There are good ones and bad ones, there are those that got into their field for the right reasons and those that didn't, and there are those who are prone to taking advantage of people just like there are those who are good hearted, ethical, and passionate. It is important to point out here that just because everyone seems to have a one-time-this-attorney-tried-to-screw-me story doesn't mean there are a disproportionate number of bad attorneys. But just like with auto mechanics, the power dynamic between customer and practitioner is such that a bad egg can become emboldened by "getting away with it" and still prospering. Again, the astute chiropractor puts this information in their back pocket and uses it as the justification for taking reasonable precautions to avoid becoming a victim rather than swearing off of personal injury cases altogether.

Chapter 7

What Chiropractors Need to Know About Insurance Before Accepting New Patients

Alexander C. Eisner: Insurance for personal injury is complicated and falls squarely under the purview of the personal injury attorney. A good personal injury attorney will be able to understand all of the myriad insurance issues fully and should be able to easily explain the specifics and details of how insurance works in any given situation. That said, here are the basics.

There are two separate types of insurance at play in most personal injury cases: Third-party insurance and first-party insurance. Third-party insurance belongs to the person who was responsible for the accident. This is usually the insurance policy attorneys are going after in their personal injury cases.

Defendants (Third-Party Insurance)

According to every state's laws (except Virginia and New Hampshire), everyone has to have auto insurance. The minimum policy in California is a "15/30 policy," which means $15,000 for any single person's bodily injury and $30,000 total for an entire incident. California also requires a minimum of $5,000 to cover property damage done to another vehicle. Some states (e.g., Florida) only require $10,000 of bodily injury coverage, while other states (e.g., Michigan) require $50,000 per person of bodily injury coverage and $100,000 per occurrence.

As an example, let's say someone (D_1) rear-ends a car while the owner (P_1) and a friend (P_2) are inside. In California, it's probable that the driver of the car that hit the victim's car (D_1) has a 15/30 policy (because it is the cheapest policy they can get and legally drive in CA). If the driver (D_1) does have such a policy, each person (P_1 <u>and</u> P_2) could get up to $15,000 out of that policy (known as the "policy limits"). However, if there were three or more people in the car that was hit, the $30,000 would be split up between them according to their amounts of damage. In the case of more than two Plaintiffs, no single Plaintiff can recover more than the individual policy limit (here, $15,000).

Plaintiffs (First-Party Insurance)

In California (as with most other states), there is the option of purchasing something called **uninsured or underinsured motorist coverage**, which covers a driver who gets into an accident that is not the their fault with a person who is either uninsured (which is illegal) or underinsured (which is very common).

To return to the case of the rear-end collision above, let's say P_1's car was hit by D_1 who has a $15,000 policy (the minimum policy a driver is legally allowed to have in CA), but D_1 caused $50,000 worth of bodily injury damages (i.e., medical bills, lost wages, compensation for pain and suffering). If P_1 has underinsured motorist coverage, P_1 must first get the $15,000 policy limit from the third-party coverage (D_1's insurance) but then can collect from their own underinsured motorist policy. That policy enjoys a "credit" in the amount recovered from the third-party policy (meaning you subtract the third-party policy limit from P_1's underinsured policy limit). So, after P_1 recovers the third-party policy limit of $15,000, P_1 can go after the $35,000 that remains in their underinsured motorist policy ($50,000 - $15,000 = $35,000).

It's important to know the details here because attorneys often try to stretch the meaning of minimal coverage. They may say, "Well, if it's a minimal policy, then the client doesn't need that much treatment." Of course, it's not that simple. A person still might need a great deal of treatment. We've had many cases where people had no first-party coverage but were hit while riding a motorcycle and sustained hundreds of thousands of dollars in bodily injury damage through no fault of their own. If the person at fault had only a 15/30 policy, all the client can get is $15,000. Again, this does not mean that the client *needs* only $15,000 worth of treatment. It just means that there's only $15,000 worth of insurance money available.

The amount of insurance available in a case is a big factor to consider when determining whether or not to take a case on lien. We will discuss liens later in this book, but for introductory purposes, liens are contracts that a chiropractor enters into with both the patient and the patient's attorney. The contract essentially says that the chiropractor will perform treatment on credit and expects to be paid out of the proceeds of the settlement or any other award when the patient's personal injury case resolves.

When chiropractors consider whether to take a case on a lien, they are also assessing how much treatment they can put on the lien. That doesn't mean how much treatment the patient needs; it means how much treatment the chiropractor can afford to put on a lien; the first decision is based on a medical assessment and the second on a risk assessment.

This estimation involves a certain amount of gambling. Every time chiropractors take a lien, they're gambling. If the case doesn't pay out, chiropractors "eat" the cost of the treatment,[5] as well as the time that could have been spent earning money through billable treatment hours. Therefore, it is incredibly important to know what sort of insurance policies are involved in each case and to factor that information into the decision-making process.

As an example, let's say the chiropractor finds out that the third party only has a $15,000 policy and that the patient, unfortunately, has no underinsured

---

[5] It is theoretically possible to enforce a lien against a patient in the absence of any civil settlement/verdict/award, but this is seldom done and difficult to achieve without suing one's own patient.

motorist coverage. This means that there is only $15,000 that could be claimed in total, assuming the suit will not go after the defendant personally.[6]

In that case, chiropractors may only be able to put a couple thousand dollars' worth of treatment on lien before they then have to convert that patient to a cash patient and (if it is financially feasible for the patient to do so) continue treatment in that way. It is not financially viable for a chiropractor to get stuck in a situation where a person is continuing to promise payment from a settlement that will never be received. This is what happens when the amount of treatment put on lien exceeds the highest possible payout for the patient. In that situation, regardless of how well the case goes, even if the patient gets the full policy limit of $15,000, there is not going to be enough money

---

[6] Technically speaking, a personal injury attorney doesn't have to accept the insurance money and can, instead, proceed against the defendant personally. Unless the defendant is independently wealthy (which is almost never the case for defendants who aren't carrying enough insurance), this is usually a fool's errand. Enforcing a judgment against an insolvent defendant is almost always not worth the effort.

available to pay the chiropractor. As a businessperson, it is not viable for a chiropractor to be in the situation of offering services with no chance of being paid.

Shawn Steel: That's what I call "running a free clinic," and as I've said before, no one wants to run a free clinic.

Alexander C. Eisner: Thank you, Shawn. When it comes to ensuring payment, it once again becomes clear why it is so important to work with a pro-chiropractic attorney. Attorneys know that if a client has a $15,000 policy, that's the maximum amount that can be obtained in a case. In these cases, the more money in medical bills the patient racks up, the easier it's going to be for the attorney to convince the insurance company to pay out the full policy limit. For example, if a client racks up $20,000 in medical bills and the attorney knows there's a $15,000 policy limit, they also know the insurance company is likely to roll over and pay the full $15,000 immediately because there's no chance that the company is going to be able to negotiate down from $15,000 when the medical bills alone, without any compensation for pain and suffering or general damages, already exceed the policy limit. Allowing or encouraging medical costs to rise to that amount is simply lazy attorneying.

In other words, if an attorney doesn't manage the case or the treatments (particularly, treatments being done on a lien), the medical bills can add up very quickly. In this situation, the lazy attorney has done nearly no work and obtained the full policy limit simply by letting the client rack up more bills than the available insurance could possibly cover. However, once the lazy attorney gets the $15,000 policy payout and takes their fee, they are left with approximately $10,000 to pay $20,000 worth of medical bills. This forces the medical practitioners involved, including chiropractors, to accept much less than their full fees. This disenfranchises hard-working medical professionals, especially the ones attorneys may have convinced to work on a lien. Without a pro-chiropractic attorney, chiropractors can easily find themselves being short-changed in this way.

Then there's the way ethical attorneys do things. It is not as easy as the method explained above, but it is certainly the more rewarding and more esteemed method. We believe it is important to closely manage care on our cases, making sure that no medical provider ends up with a lien that's going to require them to take a huge pay cut when the case resolves. In our practice, we take special care to manage these elements of our cases with chiropractors. This means maintaining open lines of dialogue so that we can tell chiropractors how much insurance money there is and allow them to adjust how much treatment they can offer on lien accordingly. Depending on the case, we check in with them at the beginning of treatment as well as at four months or six months to see what the bill looks like, as well as to see how the treatment is working out. By the end of that process, patients involved in cases with a $15,000 policy limit may end up with total medical bills of $7,000 or $8,000, rather than a bill for far more.

At that point, my job is to convince an insurance company to pay out the $15,000 policy. The company is going to fight with me and is not going to roll over and pay me $15,000 immediately on $7,000 in medical bills, as it likely would on $20,000 in medical bills. However, with a little bit of elbow grease, I can often convince the insurance company that even though there are only, for example, three providers and $7,000 in treatment, it should pay the $15,000 because my client is being treated conservatively; the injuries are real and well documented; the residual damages are moderate and, again, well documented; and ultimately the case is worth it. If I am successful, I can then pay some or all of the medical providers (especially the chiropractor) the total amount of their charges.

To me, the most important provider to pay in full is the chiropractor, simply because of how minimal their per-visit bills often are and how hard they're ultimately working for their minimal average daily fee (which is a concept we'll get into later).

Shawn Steel: Alex and I make sure to speak with every chiropractor with whom we are beginning a personal injury case. Part of our job is to give doctors an overall bird's-eye view of the potential insurance considerations of the case. If there are multiple injured people with lots of attorneys and minimal insurance, we advise them of that fact. If it turns out that there is a very large insurance policy, we advise the doctors of that fact, as well. If the case is a hardship case, where there are serious life-changing injuries but there isn't much insurance money, we let them know about that. We also let them know if the case involves a very serious injury and there is a great deal of insurance available, because this fortunately allows the patient to get the very specialized care necessary for a full recovery and likely get all of their treatment paid for through their PI case.

Chiropractors deserve to know this information from the outset so that they can determine whether it is feasible for them to take the case and can offer treatment on lien. The attorney's job is to help the chiropractor and the patient navigate the optimal care plan for the money that's available.

Alexander C. Eisner: That's literally what I just said.

Shawn Steel: We also inform our partner chiropractors about the potential liability of clients in personal injury cases. A good personal injury case is one in which the injured party is not liable (at fault) for the accident or injury. If a personal injury Plaintiff is ruled to be liable, it can significantly reduce the potential settlement and the amount of insurance money available to the Plaintiff. This is information chiropractors should have to determine whether or not to take a case.

Over ninety percent of the time, we find all the information we need to prove that a client is or isn't liable in the police report (or traffic collision report). This is another reason why it's essential to obtain police reports for personal injury cases. The reports are often riddled with errors, but they are often considered accurate by insurance companies. They may contain errors, but they are useful for fact checking. The first thing we do as personal injury attorneys is to read the police report and confirm that what the client/patient told us about the accident is corroborated in the report. We then share our findings, as well as the police report, immediately with the client's chiropractor. Most medical practitioners never look at the police report in these cases, and consequently, they're stuck flying blind on the word of the patient and the word of the attorney. Once we've shared our information, the chiropractor has our word in addition to the findings of the police report. They can examine the information themselves and use all of it to decide whether or not to take a case.

In some cases, chiropractors decide to take questionable cases with higher risk in which liability could go either way. They may take the case and work hard on it, only to find out too late in the game that the patient was partly responsible for the accident. This is rather common, as many states have a legal policy called comparative liability. Comparative liability means that personal injury settlements are tied to the claimant's liability, or responsibility, for the accident. If the patient is considered to be fifty percent in the wrong, the patient gets fifty percent of the award. That means the payout for the medical fee is likely to be only fifty percent of what was originally anticipated.[7]

When chiropractors take on these cases, they have to be aware of that possibility. Many chiropractors aren't, and are disappointed and surprised when they get less payment than they anticipated. I don't like disappointments or surprises in personal injury. Most chiropractors cannot afford to run a free clinic, and to some extent, that is what happens if they take on a risky case.

In the end, most chiropractors spend half of their time healing and the other half running a business like everybody else. As a chiropractor, running a business includes making sure that a

---

[7] Legally speaking, just because a patient got hit with fifty percent comparative negligence doesn't mean the patient's bill *has* to be reduced by fifty percent. After all, the lien entitles the chiropractor to payment in full regardless of the outcome of the case. That said, it is very difficult to get paid in such cases because there is so much less money to go around.

patient's available insurance money and potential liability are lined up in such a way that the chiropractor will be paid for services rendered.

CHAPTER 8

MEDPAY AND PERSONAL INJURY PROTECTION AND HOW THEY WORK

Shawn Steel: In the United States, each state has a different set of rules for insurance. In California, MedPay is an optional, supplemental type of insurance available to people who are also buying mandatory car insurance. It is meant to provide extra funds for treatment and recovery if injuries are sustained in an accident. It functions as additional coverage tacked onto an auto insurance policy. If a person has MedPay and gets in an accident, whether or not the person has caused it, the person now has a pool of money that was paid for in advance and that can be exclusively used to pay medical costs. It's like a mini—health insurance policy that kicks in when someone is in an accident to allow immediate treatment for things a regular health insurance policy may not cover. Importantly, it gives patients greater freedom of choice over their healthcare providers in the immediate aftermath of an accident.

Personal Injury Protection (PIP) is essentially the same thing and is offered in different jurisdictions. PIP may also cover other losses such as lost wages. PIP policies are non-reimbursable. This means that once PIP money is paid out, the PIP insurance carrier cannot assert a lien or claim for reimbursement out of the Personal Injury case settlement. This is contrasted with MedPay which only covers qualifying medical and funeral expenses and is reimbursable, usually at a two-thirds rate.

MedPay/PIP is available in different policy increments. There is $1,000 coverage, $5,000 coverage, and $100,000 coverage. None of the policies are particularly expensive. In fact, MedPay actually has one of the best cost—benefit ratios for medical insurance anywhere in the country.

Unfortunately, many people don't understand how effective and efficient MedPay is, and how it is actually a very important and financially sound investment. This lack of information is not an accident: Insurance companies are not particularly interested in promoting MedPay/PIP, since it is more beneficial for the consumer than it is for the insurance company on average. As such, enrollment rates are relatively low. Rates for MedPay in California haven't increased substantially in years, mostly because there are fewer and fewer claims let alone cases going to trial.

So, in the current insurance landscape, insurance companies continue making a tremendous amount of money on claims of all sorts that are less beneficial to the consumer but are still very efficient in discouraging people from buying MedPay. **We**

strongly urge all patients of chiropractors—and all motorists in general—to buy MedPay/PIP as soon as possible, long before they ever have an accident. It's a great investment not just for themselves but for their families as well, since MedPay follows the car rather than the individual.

As an example of how it works, let's say a driver has a $5,000 MedPay policy. One day, the driver and five cousins are in the car and get into an accident. With a $5,000 policy, that's $30,000 worth of insurance ($5,000 x 1 driver and 5 cousins), since everybody in that car gets covered at the full policy limit regardless of who caused the accident. If all six people then begin treating with a different chiropractor of their choosing—let's say they each do 40 visits over four months at an average of $125 per visit—those six chiropractors can bill the MedPay and begin getting pay contemporaneously with the treatment. They don't have to wait for a personal injury attorney to settle a case. They don't have to worry about having their bill reduced or negotiated by an attorney (though some MedPay carriers, as will be discussed in the next chapter, will attempt to cut your bill). This example makes it easy to see how it can be very useful to have that kind of insurance on a car both for your patients but also for you. It essentially takes all the risk out of handling personal injury claims.

The monthly payments on MedPay/PIP are relatively cheap and therefore make the policies widely available. In many parts of California, for example, the payment for a $5,000 MedPay policy is $5 to $10 a month. In addition, the policy offers great coverage for situations far beyond simple car accidents.

As another example of how far-reaching MedPay/PIP coverage is: Let's say an aunt is living with her niece for a few months. The aunt doesn't use the family car, opting to take the bus instead. If the bus is in an accident, or the aunt falls down and gets hurt on the bus, the MedPay policy extends to her and any other relative who is living in the policy owner's home (even if only temporarily). [8]

---

[8] This applies to nearly all MedPay policies. Individual policies may vary.

Alexander C. Eisner: In summation, chiropractors should be active advocates for MedPay/PIP, speaking with every single one of their patients about these policies for the simple reason that they decrease all the risks to chiropractors in taking on personal injury cases to nearly zero. MedPay/PIP allows chiropractors to get paid while they are treating a personal injury patient. No lien means no waiting to get paid and no potential to get screwed (unless an attorney attempts to intercept the MedPay payment, which we will discuss later).

Now, within the broader concept of MedPay, there are actually two types. There's regular, old-fashioned MedPay, and then there's something called Excess MedPay.

Standard MedPay

As we said above, MedPay works like a mini–supplemental health insurance policy. Here are some examples of how it works.

- **MedPay pays for medical visits.** Let's say a person has a health insurance policy and also a $5,000 MedPay policy. The person gets into an accident and needs the help of a chiropractor. The person goes to the chiropractor for 20 visits at a total cost of $2,000. The person then submits the bills for those 20 visits to MedPay, or the chiropractor submits them, and the chiropractor gets paid directly.
- **MedPay covers copays, deductibles, and out-of-network visits.** Let's say a person is injured in a car accident and goes to the emergency room. The person has an insurance policy with a $1,000 deductible. A person with an active MedPay policy can submit the deductible or any copays to MedPay for coverage. In addition, MedPay pays for treatments outside of a patient's usual network of providers, such as specialists, acupuncturists, physical therapists, and of course, chiropractors.

As you can see, a standard MedPay/PIP policy can be incredibly helpful for getting treatment immediately. Additionally, because it does not involve payments on a lien, it's excellent from both the patient's perspective and the chiropractor's perspective. In a personal injury case where someone gets a settlement for damages, having one less set of bills to pay from that settlement lets the patient keep money for its intended use (e.g., pain and suffering, future care, and lost wages). It is excellent for the chiropractor because, as stated, it takes all of the risk out of treating a patient, as the chiropractor is assured of being paid in full so long as the MedPay policy is sufficient. Instead of worrying about the viability of a patient's personal injury case, the chiropractor just has to worry about treating the patient. What's more, MedPay payments are usually made much quicker than payments on a lien and are much less likely to be negotiated down.

Excess MedPay

Excess MedPay is a special type of MedPay (read: scam) that was developed by insurance companies looking to increase their cut. It only kicks in once a primary health insurance policy has been exhausted. A policy holder must go through the primary health insurance company (and its in-network providers) first before Excess MedPay will pay for anything else.

For example, let's say a patient relies on the Kaiser health care system and its insurance and also has an Excess MedPay policy. If the patient's Kaiser policy does not cover chiropractic treatment, the chiropractor still has to submit a bill to Kaiser. Because Kaiser refuses to cover the chiropractor's expenses, Kaiser will send the chiropractor a Certificate of No Coverage (or some sort of letter refusing coverage). The chiropractor will have to submit that certificate or letter to the Excess MedPay carrier, which will then usually cover the treatment.

In my opinion, Excess MedPay is a little bit of a scam. In addition to the bureaucratic hurdles, the coverage from Excess MedPay is far less extensive than the coverage from standard MedPay. I have spoken to many Excess MedPay clients who believed they were getting standard MedPay benefits when they purchased Excess MedPay, but then found out the hard way that this was not so.

I generally advise that patients and clients invest in standard MedPay and avoid Excess MedPay.

CHAPTER 9

WHEN THIRD PARTIES GET INVOLVED IN DELAYING, DISCOUNTING, OR DENYING MEDPAY CLAIMS

Shawn Steel: MedPay is designed to help a motorist deal with unforeseen medical bills. Insurance companies often try to claim that unforeseen medical treatments are unnecessary expenses and try to avoid paying for them by what I call the 3Ds: Delaying, discounting, and denying.

These actions are bluffs. Insurance companies know that when they take these actions, they risk lawsuits, specifically first-party bad-faith lawsuits. They are based on the fundamental injustice of patients paying money every month for a service, medical insurance, and then not being able to get their bills paid when the time comes to use that service. Surprisingly, insurance company bluffs work a lot of the time.

In addition to first-party bad-faith suits, as well as embarrassingly bad publicity, these actions put insurance companies at risk of a special type of MedPay denial lawsuit that has been practiced in California since the 2000s. I led an effort to bring this type of lawsuit against the California State Automobile Association (CSAA) some time ago. CSAA was denying MedPay claims for their customers in Northern California, and we put together a fantastic group of lawyers and medical practitioners who opposed the CSAA actions. We eventually got the case to the District Attorney of San Francisco, and he led a consumer fraud action against CSAA, which caused the association to change its behavior. It cost the CSAA a lot of money, and a 'mass tort' case decision was made against the association, which left it quite vulnerable.

Chiropractors should keep these things in mind when insurance companies flat out refuse payment, claiming they don't think the treatment given was reasonable or necessary. Medical professionals know what a crazy bill looks like and what a reasonable bill looks like. When insurance companies start denying, delaying, or attempting to discount very reasonable bills, they know they're doing something risky, but they anticipate that a chiropractor will not call their bluff.

In these cases, if chiropractors continue to get denials, delays, and attempts to discount fees for unfounded reasons (or no reasons at all), we suggest working with an ethical, pro-chiropractic attorney. A good attorney will effectively and efficiently call an insurance company's bluff. Often this takes the form of writing a demand letter on behalf of the chiropractor and giving the insurance company a deadline by which to pay the fees in full. This basically lets the company know that the chiropractor means business and that the company now must choose to either pay the fees or face a Bad Faith lawsuit. This might sound drastic, but it often only takes one such instance before a company learns that a chiropractor isn't messing around when it comes to MedPay.

Chiropractors often face situations in which an insurance company refuses to honor a legitimate bill and stops communicating, often despite the fact that there is plenty of available MedPay coverage. In these cases, one of my favorite and most effective tactics is to sue the insurance company in small claims court. This incurs far more costs and requires more time and effort for the insurance company than the denial of the claim incurred in the first place, and it usually results in successful recompense for my clients (see Appendix C: MedPay Collection Kit).

Ultimately, an ethical attorney has an obligation to fight for their clients' MedPay benefits and assist chiropractors in getting paid.

What Chiropractors Should Do if an Attorney Attempts to Intercept a MedPay Payment

Shawn Steel: Unfortunately, attorneys sometimes act unethically when it comes to MedPay. One way they do this is to circumvent the chiropractor and have the check for the entire MedPay payment (usually around $5,000) made out to the attorney. It is fairly easy for an attorney to write a letter requesting this payment circumvention.

This can leave chiropractors high and dry. For instance, let's say a chiropractor treats a patient over the course of a month, including with an initial exam and x-rays, and the bill is around $1,000. The chiropractor submits the bill to the patient's MedPay insurance company and is told that the company has already issued payment to the attorney. Or worse still, the MedPay insurance company may accept the bill and issue payment directly to the attorney rather than to the doctor at the attorney's request. At that point, the attorney may or may not decide to share the funds owed to the chiropractor with the chiropractor. This is done so that the attorney can negotiate and reduce the medical liens from providers that rightly billed the MedPay in the first place and either pass the savings onto the patient or take a fee partly out of the MedPay money (or both).

This practice is very unethical, but it is unfortunately quite widespread. If it does happen and an attorney is intentionally withholding funds and/or refusing to communicate about them, the chiropractor's working relationship with the attorney should end immediately. The chiropractor should counsel their patient to consider hiring a better, more ethical attorney to take over. The new attorney can sue to force the old attorney's hand and get the funds the chiropractor deserves, which are likely being kept in the unethical attorney's client trust account.

Alexander C. Eisner: Shawn and I happen to disagree on how bad this practice is and how severely it should be punished. I go so far as to say that it does actually break laws and amounts to insurance fraud and should therefore be considered illegal. My evidence is the fact that every single MedPay contract specifies that the payments are only to be used for "qualified medical treatment and funeral expenses." Those are the only two permissible uses for MedPay. If attorneys were to be honest with the insurance company in their letter, they would have to specify that they intend to use the payment being handed over to them for both medical treatment <u>and</u> legal services rendered (and, if there are any leftovers, for the client for pain and suffering). If an attorney did that, such a request would be denied, because legal expenses are not covered under MedPay (nor is pain and suffering).

That fundamental dishonesty is where I think the claim for insurance fraud can be made. These unethical attorneys intentionally deceive insurance companies so they will make MedPay payments to them, under the guise that they will be using them exclusively to pay medical providers for their services. Instead, they either keep all of the payment or take a larger-than-agreed-upon fee from it, usually at the expense of the medical providers the funds were supposed to pay. Often, these attorneys forcibly reduce the chiropractor's fees themselves. They do so artificially, as they were usually given enough money by the insurance company to pay the chiropractor's bill in full (as intended).

For example, if a chiropractor submits a bill for $2,000 to MedPay and then MedPay gives the intercepting attorney the $2,000 payment, the intercepting attorney often tells the chiropractor that only $1,000 of the chiropractor's bill will be paid from the payment the attorney received. Sometimes attorneys claim that the insurance company only paid that much, and sometimes they don't offer any explanation at all. In any case, it leaves the intercepting attorney with $1,000 of MedPay money in a client trust account. Attorneys can decide to do several things with that money, including giving it all to the client, keeping part of it as payment for attorneys' fees and giving the client the rest, paying other medical bills with it, or keeping the entire $1,000 for themselves. In any case, the money was rightfully meant for and should have been given to the chiropractor who billed it in payment for medical services rendered (as outlined in the bill that the attorney likely had to submit to the MedPay provider to justify the money in the first place). Had the MedPay insurance company known that the money was not going to be used for the appropriate payments, the money would not have been issued to the attorney. **Any time there is a situation in which honesty on the part of an attorney when dealing with an insurance company would have caused the company <u>not</u> to pay a claim, one can be pretty sure that it is a fraudulent situation.**

The offending attorneys, of course, disagree. I recently encountered this disagreement when I wrote an article on the subject for the journal *Dynamic Chiropractic,*[9] which essentially said that I think the practice amounts to insurance fraud. I got a lot of angry emails from attorneys who insisted I was wrong, though they couldn't quite explain how or why. One even went so far as to say that if he refers a person to a

---

9 https://www.dynamicchiropractic.com/digital/index.php?i=1269&a_id=58758&pn=31&r=t&Page=31

chiropractor for treatment, he forbids that chiropractor from billing MedPay and requires the chiropractor to allow him (the attorney) to intercept MedPay payments on the chiropractor's behalf and that he considers this a "way [for the chiropractor] to say thank you for the referral." The attorney who does this is not only committing insurance fraud but is accepting an illegal kickback!

So, while there is a difference of opinion on the subject, Shawn and I both believe that any attorney that steals or intercepts MedPay payments is doing something unethical at the very least. Bottom line: If an attorney does this to a chiropractor, the chiropractor should advise their patient that they can't work with that attorney, and that if they want to continue treatment on a lien, they should find a new attorney who will relinquish the funds as intended.

CHAPTER 10

MAKING REASONABLE AND NECESSARY REFERRALS

Shawn Steel: According to the California Board of Chiropractic Examiners, Rules and Regulations, it is absolutely mandatory to refer patients out to other medical professionals and specialists if their diagnosis, symptoms, and necessary treatments are outside of the chiropractor's scope.[10] Serious trauma cases almost always require triage care.

The question of what is inside or outside of a chiropractor's scope can be somewhat vague. Trauma often causes multisystem injuries that impact multiple areas of the body, as well as the mind. Trauma injuries therefore often require multiple specialists and accommodations for both physical and psychological treatment. In a serious trauma case, it is absolutely recommended and usually required to refer the patient to the appropriate specialists. This is all done in the interest of getting patients the best possible care. Chiropractic cases often have co-consultations with orthopedists and orthopedic surgeons, neurologists neuropsychiatrists and neuropsychologists, trauma therapists, and physical therapists, among others.

Accurate imaging is crucial to chiropractic practice. Chiropractors have been at the forefront of

---

[10] California Board of Chiropractic Examiners, Rules and Regulations § 317(w)

using imaging technology for many years, and the increasing access to ever-improving imaging technology has been immeasurably helpful to the field. In many chiropractic cases, especially trauma cases, imaging is crucial for giving practitioners a clear picture of what's happening to the patient's body internally, especially the spine, other musculoskeletal areas, joints, and extremities. Patients almost always need x-rays. More severe trauma cases need appropriate imaging done at an MRI center, such as standard MRIs, flexion MRIs, standing MRIs, and 3T (3.0-Tesla) brain MRIs.

If the chiropractor is continuing to manage the care of a patient, the specialist or imaging technologist reports back to the chiropractor on the findings and offers suggestions for care. The findings usually either confirm the chiropractor's initial diagnosis or counter that diagnosis and provide a new meaningful diagnosis in its place. All of this input can help chiropractors manage patients better, make smarter referrals, and offer the highest level of care.

Alexander C. Eisner: It should be noted here, as I have noted often in many lectures and conferences, that these consults and referrals take nothing away from the chiropractor. It is more than acceptable, and in fact is a testament to medical validity and strength, for chiropractors to admit that there are situations that are outside of the scope of their practice and that other specialists may be better suited to treat. Unfortunately, I have met chiropractors who do not want to relinquish the control of a patient to another specialist, even when it's the right thing to do. This is a mistake (and in some instances, a form of malpractice) and does not serve either the chiropractor or the patient.

Referrals out to specialists are helpful in almost any potential personal injury case because the additional input helps to bolster a patient's diagnosis (whether it's the chiropractor's original diagnosis or a different diagnosis) and also helps to substantiate the treatment plans. If chiropractors do not have imaging machines in their offices, they should refer patients out to an imaging specialist and make sure they document why that was a necessity. This sort of referral and documentation are required under the rules and regulations of the Board of Chiropractic Examiners in California.[11] They are also important from a personal injury perspective, because the more justification a chiropractor has for all aspects of patient treatment, the less successful insurance companies will be in trying to get out of paying for them.

Does It Matter Who a Chiropractor Refers a Patient To? Is There Such a Thing as Over-referring or Under-referring?

Alexander C. Eisner: Yes, it matters who patients are referred to, and yes, it is possible to over-refer or under-refer patients.

There are a few reasons why it matters who patients are referred to. Chiropractors want to make sure their patients are going to qualified, highly regarded medical practitioners, technicians, and specialists so they will have the best possible care.

---

[11] CA Board of Chiropractic Examiners, Rules and Regulations, § 312 1-4, § 317(d).

It also matters because chiropractors want to send patients to practitioners who are pro-chiropractic. Sometimes, chiropractors send patients to anti-chiropractic specialists and practitioners, who then turn the patients against them. For instance, let's say a chiropractor sends a patient to a personal injury medical center for an evaluation. If the patient encounters an anti-chiropractic specialist there, the specialist may convince the patient that chiropractic is bunk and steal the patient away. The specialist then sends the patient to a trauma physician affiliated with the specialist's practice rather than having the patient continue to see the chiropractor. I've also seen situations where a chiropractor entrusts a patient to an orthopedist, who then writes in a report that the chiropractic treatment was unnecessary or even made the patient's situation or injury worse. It is incredibly important that chiropractors choose people who are known to be pro-chiropractic, as well as ethical, people who are not going to proceed with surgery just for the sake of doing surgery or prescribe drugs as an easy way out.

If chiropractors don't know of a good practitioner in a certain subspecialty, they should be able to ask their personal injury attorney for a recommendation. For instance, if a chiropractor is working with us and has a pregnant client who was in an accident and needs a specialist in OB/GYN, the chiropractor should be able to say, "Hey, Shawn and Alex, I need a pro-chiropractic OB/GYN trauma specialist." Good attorneys have a list of subspecialists who have been pre-vetted and referred to in the past that can be shared with chiropractors.

As for under-referring or over-referring, these can both be issues. Under-referring often happens in cases like the ones we mentioned previously, in which chiropractors become hesitant to refer their patients out to other specialists or do not properly identify the signs that a specialist is needed.

Chiropractors can also over-refer. If there is a diagnostic clue such as a headache on the day of an accident, a referral for a neurocognitive workup, psychologist, and family therapist isn't necessarily required. This would be grossly over-referring based on the number of symptoms, and it would be questioned when it comes time to justify the bill. Remember, insurance companies are only required to pay for "reasonable and necessary" treatment.

So if, for example, chiropractors refer a patient for an MRI without documenting any medical necessity, the insurance company is probably going to claim that the referral was not reasonable and necessary, and they're not going to pay for it. For that reason, documenting medical necessity and then referring patients to appropriate subspecialists is incredibly important.

Why Is It Important for Chiropractors to Build Referral Relationships with Physicians in Their Community?

Shawn Steel: I tell all our students that one of the first things they need to do as chiropractors is to start building a personal medical triage network. That's an important concept. I think most of the younger chiropractors understand that comprehensive care is really what patients want. They don't want one choice; they want to have the maximum care they can get, with multiple different angles of treatment, and a well-connected chiropractor is precisely who they're looking for. When I say well-connected, what I mean is somebody that has good peer-to-peer relationships with medical doctors and specialists in the community.

Establishing and building those relationships means going out of the way to find pro-chiropractic doctors and medical professionals and reaching out to them to network. This sort of network building can start at any time in a person's life or career. It is just a matter of establishing allies and forming a community centered around patient care.

It should be noted that the younger generation of doctors seems well-suited to forming relationships and communities with chiropractors. They are more sensitive and appreciative of what a chiropractor does. Some "old school" doctors tend to be wary of working with chiropractors, though not all of them feel this way. In any case, chiropractors should make sure to seek out medical professionals who are at least curious about chiropractic and who want to see how chiropractors get their outcomes and successes.

There are a number of ways of finding doctors and medical professionals in the community. Sometimes they reach out to chiropractors, but it's better that chiropractors reach out to them. A chiropractor should know the other chiropractors in the local community (with or without external networking). Chiropractors can share information on which doctors in the community are good to work with. They know from experience whether they had good or bad interactions with individual doctors and medical practitioners.

Chiropractors can also do this networking through pro-chiropractic personal injury attorneys. For example, I have a comprehensive list of doctors in California that provide personal injury medical care. Each medical professional is rated by how the professional relates to chiropractic practice (either positively, negatively, or neutrally), as well as the professional's reputation and competency. I'm happy to share my findings with any doctor that needs them.

Yet another source of information on doctors and medical professionals that would be good to network with is patients. Even if patients are seeking a chiropractor's help, they may be also working with medical professionals who they know to be amenable to chiropractic help. These are good doctors and medical practitioners to know.

Some chiropractors say they don't have time to network. To them I say, it would be good to make the time. If a younger chiropractor is just starting out, the beginning period of practice is the best time to do this. In the first six months of practice, when the chiropractor is just opening the door, there is a period of time in which the chiropractor is building a clientele and the practice schedule isn't too hurried. During that time, the chiropractor should make plans to sit down and have lunch with medical doctors who have personal injury experience in the community.

Chiropractors don't need to know every single personal injury doctor in the world, or even in the community. All they really need to start out are two or three good connections with personal injury medical practitioners, since each one will have a network that they will share if things go well.

Having the network to help patients get referrals to the right practitioners makes a huge difference. Making smart referrals lends chiropractors a great deal of credibility. Let's say that a patient sees a chiropractor for a back injury but also has an eye problem. If the chiropractor is able to refer the patient to an optometrist with personal injury experience, the patient will be grateful and will always want to go back for similar feedback and resources.

In short, one of the keys to building a career as a successful chiropractor is being able to make the right referrals. This will also help chiropractors to get cases through referrals from the other medical practitioners in the network. A chiropractor who does this will become established in the community as the chiropractor who makes additional efforts on behalf of patients.

CHAPTER 11

MAINTAINING PATIENT CONFIDENCE AND COMPLIANCE

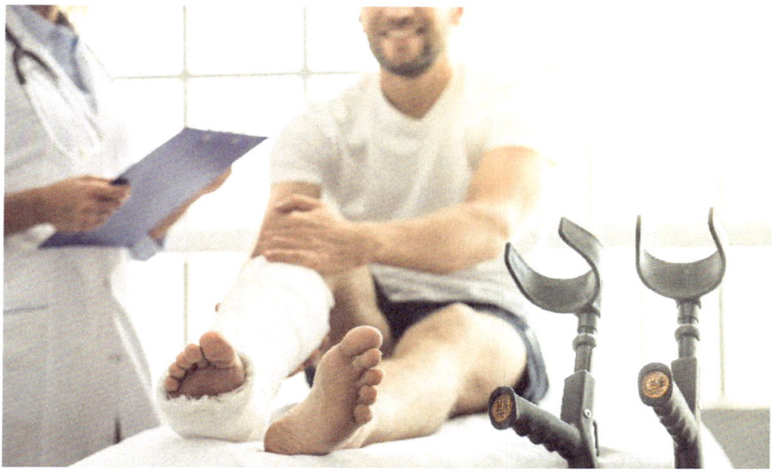

Alexander C. Eisner: One of the most essential things to try to establish at the beginning of a relationship with a patient is confidence. **Gaining patient confidence leads to gaining patient compliance.** One of the easiest ways of gaining patient confidence and compliance is by being an authority on the subjects chiropractors should know about, such as personal injury and healing the body from trauma, and discussing them clearly.

Another way to gain patient confidence and compliance is by doing what one says one is going to do. For instance, if a chiropractor tells a patient that a series of appointments will be set up over a certain span of time, make sure the appointments are set up in that way and be present for them. Give patients worthwhile goals on a realistic timeline. That is, let them know when they should be able to expect a certain level of healing or pain reduction, but only if the timeline is realistic. This goes a long way in building credibility and ultimately building compliance.

Compliance is an important concept in these cases. There are many times in personal injury where patient compliance becomes difficult to establish and maintain. This can become a sensitive subject, but it is crucial to getting the patient to do something. This could be coming into the office for an examination so a final report can be completed, or getting a patient to sign a form or letter, or getting a patient to do at-home exercises. These are all matters of compliance. I've found that the more compliant clients are the ones that have great working relationships with their chiropractors and have been shown, not told, that the chiropractor is the authority on the subject of the client's recovery and treatment.

How Often Should Chiropractors Educate Their Patients About What They Are Doing?

Alexander C. Eisner: Doctors of Chiropractic should consult and educate their patients at every visit. The education of patients is essential, both for building confidence in chiropractic work and also for giving patients a vested interest in making sure the bill gets paid. In deposition settings, for instance, when a client cannot articulate exactly what their chiropractor did for them, it is that much more difficult for the chiropractor to justify the expenses. I can personally attest to many occasions in depositions where Plaintiffs (patients) are asked what a chiropractor did for them and they respond by talking about heating pads and attempting to explain what a TENS unit is. When a patient completes treatment with a chiropractor, there should be no one more knowledgeable about what was done for the patient than the patient. Think of every visit as an opportunity to create yet another spokesperson for the practice and for chiropractic writ large. When patients sit for a deposition, they should be able to explain exactly what the chiropractor did for them, what tools were used to accomplish it, and what they were taught to do for themselves going forward. The patient who can do that is an unwitting advocate for getting the chiropractor's bill paid (both in a deposition, as well as in the insistence to the attorney that the chiropractor be paid in full).

Into Which Areas of a Patient's Life Should Chiropractors Probe During Recovery?

Alexander C. Eisner: Chiropractors spend more time with their patients than anybody else within the personal injury sphere. During that time, they should be asking a whole myriad of questions about life circumstances, activities of daily living, economics, mental health, and general well-being. These things can often lead to additional recommendations for treatment and referrals. Asking these questions not only helps patients recover more fully and completely from their accidents but also helps increase the validity of their personal injury case, which increases the odds that the chiropractor's bill will get paid. It also increases the bond between patient and doctor. As the "quarterback of the case," the chiropractor should not just have a passing interest in the patient; it is the chiropractor's job to really *know* the patient so assistance can be provided in all aspects of the patient's recovery. Doctors who take this to heart often have patients who aren't just temporary consumers of chiropractic treatment but are true advocates for *their* doctor.

What Records Should Chiropractors Obtain to Get a Complete Picture of Their Patient's Condition?

Alexander C. Eisner: Chiropractors need to see a patient's emergency room records. This means not only the standard records from the ER but also the records from the intake desk, the reports of any tests done indirectly through the ER, as well as the discharge paperwork. This often includes ambulance reports, which are physically attached to the ER records, as well as police reports and pictures of the accident itself and pictures of the patient directly after the accident. Any good, self-respecting personal injury law firm will provide these things to the chiropractor immediately and without delay, but if it doesn't, the chiropractor is entitled to them and, I would argue, obligated to obtain them to do a thorough analysis of the case.

It is important to make sure that injuries are documented at the first visit, especially if the patient is being seen soon after the accident. If there are physical signs of trauma that are likely to go away, such as bruising, lacerations, and swelling, they should be documented and photographed at the first visit. Try and make sure these match up with the injuries noted by the EMTs and ER doctors who examined the patient. Mismatched information in records is a quick and easy way to give some insurance adjuster a bit of unearned ammunition against a patient's case and, by extension, against paying a chiropractor's bill. More on this topic is given below.

Are Monthly Evaluations Warranted? How Often and in What Manner Should Chiropractors Measure Pain and Inquire About Activities of Daily Living?

Shawn Steel: For moderate-to-serious trauma cases, I think it's essential to have monthly evaluations. These are fifteen-minute face-to-face examinations that can be very valuable in terms of treatment, providing the patient with comfort, and helping the chiropractor see the progress the patient is making. If the progress is slower than anticipated, the chiropractor may consider changing treatment protocols. If progress is good, the chiropractor knows what works for this patient and can continue forward.

These examinations should include a physical, and they should document what has stayed the same and what has changed, for better or for worse. Patients should also fill out a pain scale to see what level of pain they're experiencing in which parts of the body.

These exams are also a good time to review activities of daily living (ADLs). Patients can fill out an ADL worksheet while they're in the waiting room, which keeps them from feeling like they're spending most of their visit waiting for the chiropractor. ADLs are great for gleaning insights into a patient's lifestyle and how exactly their injuries have impacted their lives on a day-to-day basis. The chiropractor may learn that the patient was a semiprofessional horseback rider or had a hobby growing heirloom tomatoes until they complained of not being able to do these things in their ADL worksheet. These details may sound a little funny and awkward, but they add a lot of value to each case. This helps with the ability to treat the patient as a full human being with a complex and unique life. It also helps with the personal injury case by giving the attorney the ability to relate compelling, real-life examples of the impact the injury has had on a patient's life.

What Will the Insurance Company Be Looking for When It Comes to Comparing the Chiropractor's Report with the ER Report?

Shawn Steel: One of the main things insurance companies look for is an inconsistency between what the chiropractor says and what the ER report says. Unfortunately, chiropractors can totally blow personal injury cases by failing to grapple with prior records before writing an initial report. We have dealt with cases in the past where the chiropractor never saw the ER records, or where we got the ER records and sent them to the chiropractor but the chiropractor didn't read them. In these cases, the ER report included crucial information about serious injuries, including traumatic brain injuries and serious fractures. The chiropractors' evident failure to read the ER reports resulted in inconsistencies between their notes and the ER reports, and this sank their credibility in a personal injury context. More importantly, in addition to hindering the personal injury cases, this hindered the chiropractors' ability to deliver a high level of care. It should also be said that many ER reports are haphazard and grossly incomplete.

If chiropractors do not check on available information from other medical experts who have seen the patient in the immediate aftermath of an accident and are just looking at the physical symptoms on the day the patient comes into the office, they're not taking the holistic approach that they are ethically and legally responsible for maintaining in their practice.

So, for a number of reasons, it is crucial that there are no major contradictions between chiropractors' findings and the ER report. Now, there are many cases where chiropractors receive ER reports that they don't believe are sufficient. This often happens when ER doctors are so busy that they only do a superficial examination and miss key findings, or when a patient is in shock and therefore not a good historian. Chiropractors usually do far more in-depth examinations and have the privilege of working from the relative calm of their offices. It follows that chiropractors' reports are usually much more thorough. However, this difference is not necessarily a contradiction and is in fact usually an improvement.

For instance, sometimes an ER doctor will say that the patient did not complain of neck pain after an accident, but by the time a chiropractor sees the patient, neck pain has developed or significantly worsened. This is sometimes caused by muscle spasms that occur days after an actual injury. In this case, the chiropractor's report of a neck injury and complaints of neck pain is not contradictory to the ER report but, rather, is building on the report of the initial symptoms. A chiropractor's notes should explain that the difference between the chiropractic report and the ER report is not a contradiction but, rather, a follow-up on the condition as it evolved. The way to avoid apparent contradictions here is by incorporating and building on the information in the other reports, rather than failing to mention it or negating it.

External Inconsistences

Alexander C. Eisner: These types of external inconsistencies can occur between a chiropractor's notes and ER reports, as well as any other documentation from any other treatment of the patient by a medical professional. They can occur with a physical therapist's notes, an orthopedist's notes, or even a psychologist's notes. These are all considered equally important by insurance adjusters and defense attorneys, and any inconsistencies will be immediately flagged and used to poke holes in the plaintiff's theory of the case.

As a cautionary tale, see what a skilled defense attorney did to this chiropractor in a deposition:

Q: It is your custom and practice to note all of a patient's injuries in your report, correct?

A: All the ones they tell me about.

Q: If a patient told you about an injury or you learned of it through a medical record, you would include it in your report, right?

A: Sure.

Q: You received a subpoena to produce all of your records in this case, correct?

A: That's correct.

Q: And you complied with that, right?

A: That's right.

Q: And you signed the declaration of records form under penalty of perjury, affirming that you produced all of the records in your file, right?

A: That's right.

Q: You reviewed all of these records when they came into your office, right?

A: I reviewed them all, not necessarily right when they came into my office, but I reviewed them all.

Q: But it is your custom and practice to review all of the records that come in on your patients, right?

A: Of course.

Q: And one of the records in your file for [redacted] was this ER record, right?

A: Right.

Q: And you reviewed it just like you reviewed all of the records you received, right?

A: Right.

Q: You see here on page 3 that it says [redacted] complains of pain to their right shoulder?

A: Yes.

Q: And here on page 9 they talk about a possible rotator cuff tear. Do you see that here?

A: Ya.

Q: So you reviewed these records and did a physical examination of your patient [redacted] and checked the box for shoulder pain on your intake form, and yet nowhere in your records does it discuss [redacted]'s shoulder. Why is that?

A: Well I think [redacted] was treated for his shoulder with a pain management doctor.

Q: Doctor, your patient was treating [sic] with you 39 times. Each of your dates of service claims that a physical examination was done. None of them discuss [redacted]'s shoulder. Why didn't you include that injury in any of your reports?

A: He was treated for his shoulder with the PM and I— pre-existing problems that are being treated by another specialty I often will—I don't always—[unintelligible]

Q: Well, are there any other errors in your reports? Any other injuries that should or shouldn't have been documented?

A: Not to my knowledge.

Q: Is there any way to know for sure that your reports are correct?

A: I don't know.

I'm sure that was tough to read. If you were thinking "Why didn't you step in and help the poor doctor?" please know that once we are at this point, there's not a whole lot we can do to help. As we will discuss later, the Plaintiff's attorney legally cannot represent the chiropractor and cannot interfere on the chiropractor's behalf in a deposition setting. This particular case just boiled down to a doctor who no doubt wishes he had read the ER records and included the shoulder in his initial report (which would have likely meant that it was included in every subsequent report). Like Shawn said, blatant inconsistencies can be case killers.

Internal Inconsistencies

In addition to external inconsistencies, in which a chiropractor's notes are inconsistent with another medical report, insurance companies also look for internal inconsistencies, which are inconsistencies within the chiropractor's own treatment plan and accompanying notes.

One type of internal inconsistency is when the chiropractor's initial report, treatment notes, and final notes or discharge report aren't consistent with one another. This can be a huge problem when trying to justify treatment. For instance, let's say a chiropractor took a patient off of work for one day initially but the treatment notes for the last visit indicate that the patient has not worked during the entire time between the two visits (this is a real-life example). This often leaves chiropractors trying to backpedal and justify the difference between the initial prescription and what wound up happening.

Shawn Steel: Finally, I'd like to add a note on trauma codes. The term "ICD10 codes" refers to a medical classification list put together by the World Health Organization (WHO). This list contains over 60,000 codes for specific injuries and diseases, as well as symptoms, complaints, causes, and other factors having to do with injury and disease. These codes help medical professionals implement a more detailed protocol for examining patients and coming to diagnoses with more analytic precision.

Included in this book (see Appendix A) is a list of trauma codes put together by Sam Collins, who is an expert on ICD10 codes (which makes sense seeing as he was one of the very few people on the American delegation dispatched to the WHO to assist in drafting the codes). He has isolated 200 key trauma codes that every chiropractor ought to be aware of and have in their lexicon. The trauma codes isolate the areas that are most frequently encountered by chiropractors when treating and diagnosing a trauma patient. While billing and coding is outside the purview of this book, suffice it to say that trauma patients should be billed and coded differently to communicate to adjusters the nature of the injuries being treated.

CHAPTER 12

OFFERING THE RIGHT AMOUNT OF TREATMENT

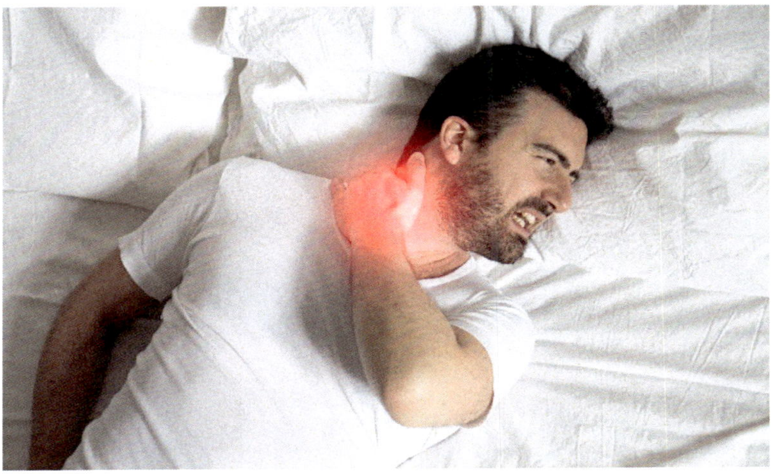

Alexander C. Eisner: There is no magic formula for the "right" amount of treatment. This is true for traumatic injuries and most non-traumatic injuries. Every case is different, and medical practitioners must work with their patients on a case-by-case basis to calculate the right amount of treatment for them. As a medical practitioner caring for a personal injury patient, it is ultimately the chiropractor's call as to how much treatment is the right amount of treatment.

However, viable personal injury cases have specific boundaries and parameters that chiropractors should be aware of.

If treatment lasts for less than three months (or less than twenty treatments) and the injury is for all intents and purposes healed, the case is very unlikely to be a substantial personal injury case. Although a quick recovery like this is excellent news for the patient, it means that the potential costs are going to be quite low in a personal injury context. If chiropractors believe at the outset that a patient will be largely or completely healed by exclusively chiropractic treatment lasting less than three months or twenty visits, they should very likely not perform such treatment on a lien. "One-doc cases" very seldom return enough money to pay a doctor's bill in full after the attorney's costs and fees have been paid and some money has been put in the patient's pocket. MedPay, insurance, or cash for these cases is preferable.

If treatment lasts more than six months (or more than sixty treatments), however, chiropractors run into problems with pushback on the efficacy of chiropractic treatment. Insurance companies may resist compensating treatment if it continues for that long without significant results. They will claim that after a while the treatment is "palliative" and no longer providing any appreciable benefit to the patient's condition. Whether that's true or not is irrelevant. If chiropractors ever find themselves in the position where they've been treating for more than six months or more than sixty visits, they should get in touch with the plaintiff's attorney. They should make sure everyone is on the same page regarding whether the case can support additional treatment on lien.

Shawn Steel: If a patient is not showing improvement after six months, the onus is on the chiropractor to further justify the care. That usually requires outside referrals, strong imaging reports, and/or aggravating circumstances in the patient's life. Otherwise, there should be substantial improvement within the first six months of treatment. There is some wiggle room for this deadline, but if a patient is still experiencing pain as an 8 out of 10 on the pain scale and six months of treatment have passed, there may be something wrong with the chiropractic protocols. By that time, the effectiveness of the care will be called into question by the personal injury community unless there are outside objective factors justifying the slow pace of progress, as well as the continuation of treatment.

As a general rule, if a patient is not making substantial progress within the first six months of treatment, chiropractors should at least look closely at their protocols and treatment methods and figure out what isn't working. They should also consider referrals to providers offering complementary therapies and treatments, including doctors with relevant medical specialties, physical therapists, acupuncturists, or maybe even another chiropractor (*gasp*).

The chiropractor's burden is to meticulously document and show that the treatment is helping the patient's healing. Documenting that progress and the necessity of the treatment is a requirement of the rules and regulations of chiropractic established by the State of California.[12] It should be noted that there are some cases that require more or less treatment than average. It is up to the chiropractor to justify why that is so in a given case.

The key to all of this is communication. Chiropractors want to make sure they're communicating with both the client and the personal injury attorney with whom they're working. This is true in any case but is especially true if they find that they're treating one patient longer than most of their other patients, or if they've been treating the patient for a longer-than-average amount of time with less improvement than would be expected. It's best to be proactive in these matters rather than reactive. Instead of waiting for pushback, if chiropractors notice that treatment is taking longer and is less effective than usual within a certain time frame, they should reach out to the personal injury attorney on the case. Let the attorney know the length and quantity of treatment, as

---

[12] Viewable at https://www.chiro.ca.gov/laws_regs/regulations.pdf

well as the patient's rate of improvement and what the current cost of that treatment is. It's acceptable to ask outright whether the case can still support continued treatment at that rate on lien.

One advantage of being forthright with your PI attorney is preventing the sticker shock when the personal injury attorney sees the bill. If the attorney is kept in the loop on expenses, it reduces potential friction with the chiropractor and generally cuts down on nasty surprises. If chiropractors want to get their bills paid in full, communication is crucial.

CHAPTER 13

ETHICAL CONSIDERATIONS IN PERSONAL INJURY

Alexander C. Eisner: In this section of the book, we've condensed the material from what is a multiple-hours-long class on ethics in personal injury. We specifically want to talk about the situations where chiropractors often get into ethical trouble, especially the ones where this happens unintentionally. There are many ways in which a person can intentionally act unethically, but we have found that the far scarier issues for chiropractors are the ways in which they might unintentionally run afoul of the chiropractic rules and standards.

The first things we want to talk about are the four major elements of insurance fraud that chiropractors may inadvertently encounter: Unbundling, upcoding, billing for services not rendered, and excessive treatment.

- **Unbundling:** Unbundling is the practice of billing separately for services that should all be included in one billing code. More than ever, the government and insurance carriers are filing cases based on the False Claims Act against practitioners. A recent example involves a physician who was using numerous billing codes to bill for each of the component parts of an epidural injection for which one billing code is supposed to encompass everything. This particular case was made worse when other insurance companies began filing the same suit against the same doctor for the same thing. The suit was initially thrown out for being duplicitous, but it was later upheld on appeal. This set a very dangerous precedent for doctors of all kinds who engage in such behavior.

- **Upcoding:** Upcoding is the practice of billing for a service that is more expensive than the one being provided. For example, if a service only requires fifteen minutes but a doctor bills for thirty minutes (without actually having spent that time), that's upcoding. Though upcoding may seem innocuous, it's serious, as it is, quite literally, insurance fraud. Generally, the people who review chiropractic bills are also chiropractors, so they know the particular procedures in question, as well as how long they take and how much they cost. Sting operations have also be used to time procedures and match these against the codes used by the doctor.

Shawn Steel: The reviewing of bills to prevent upcoding is a huge growth industry. Where in the past a bill auditor would likely let slide one or even a few 'upcodes' over time, now even one charge that seems inaccurate due to a time or severity modifier will be called out. Sometimes, if reviewers suspect a systemic problem, they will do their own investigation to gather proof before they alert the practitioner. One common tactic is to call the patient and ask how long the treatments in question took.

Alexander C. Eisner: If medical practitioners are found to be upcoding, they are flagged by the National Insurance Crime Bureau and wind up on its radar. Once practitioners have been flagged by the NICB, every case they submit from then on will be flagged, and this can cause major issues.

- **Billing for services not rendered:** This is the practice of billing for something that was not actually provided to the patient. It is distinct from upcoding because it is billing for something that is entirely fabricated rather than exaggerated. This can be an intentional act. However, many allegations of this type arise from confusion or sticker shock on the part of the patient, who is trying to make sense of a bill at the end of treatment. If a patient feels that the bill has charges for services never received, it can become a very big problem for a chiropractor.

There are a couple of ways to handle this. One is to make sure that every single patient sees a bill on a monthly basis. Chiropractors can do this by handing the patient a paper copy of the bill at the end of the visit every month. They can remind the patient that the payment is not due now but that they simply want the patient to view the bill and keep a copy for the patient's records. This cuts down on sticker shock.

Another way to handle billing is by having a robust sign-in procedure. This ensures that there is recorded, verifiable data proving that the patient came in and received services. Examples of methods commonly used by chiropractors include physical sign-in sheets, digital sign-in sheets, thumbprint systems, camera recordings (often with the camera aimed at the area where patients sign a physical sign-in sheet), and third-party witnesses.

These documentation-based measures can protect chiropractors against allegations from lying or confused patients that they are being charged for services they never received.

Lastly, it is worth reiterating that simply communicating with patients about the treatment they are receiving at every single visit can help when they later are asked whether they received some specific treatment. If the chiropractor has mentioned the treatment to the patient several dozen times, the patient is likely to remember it.

- **Excessive treatment:** Excessive treatment is a practice where a chiropractor gives a patient more treatment than is reasonably necessary. The main way to protect against allegations of excessive treatment is to be extremely thorough in the documentation of necessity (as mentioned in the previous chapter).

False or Misleading Advertising

Shawn Steel: False or misleading advertising can easily get chiropractors into a good deal of trouble, often without them realizing it. This is because the parameters of what is considered "false" or "misleading" in advertising are frequently misunderstood.

First of all, if chiropractors have a website, they need to be careful about what is on that website. For example, during the COVID-19 crisis, some chiropractors were making outlandish claims on their websites about being able to cure or prevent COVID-19. This was happening so frequently that several national chiropractic bodies had to put out an official warning against making claims of this sort. A chiropractor may be able to bolster holistic wellness, and that no doubt benefits the immune system and may increase one's ability to fight COVID-19, but it would be false and misleading advertising to claim that a chiropractor could actually cure the disease. This can also run afoul of a chiropractor's scope of practice.

Chiropractors should also be careful about the way they advertise themselves as personal injury "specialists." There is no official certification for being a specialist in personal injury, and if a chiropractor does specialize in the field, it's worth mentioning. However, in any formal context, such as a trial or deposition, that claim can be quickly turned against you. An attorney can question you further on the meaning of the term, asking if you have special training, or have privileges at an emergency room, or have a relationship with a local hospital. These questions are used to discredit the chiropractor and all the chiropractor's testimony on the stand, which, by extension, discredits the case the chiropractor is associated with (plus, the chiropractor's malpractice carrier will not be pleased).

Instead of opening themselves up to that sort of vulnerability, chiropractors can say that they accept and have experience with trauma cases. They can speak to their specialized abilities by describing their experience, without making claims they cannot prove.

Kickbacks

Alexander C. Eisner: Kickbacks are illegal and considered immoral acts of bribery. The California Chiropractic Board Rules and Regulations Section 317 on unprofessional conduct in subsection (t) states: "The offering, delivering, receiving or accepting of any rebate, refund, commission, preference, patronage, dividend, discount or other consideration as compensation or inducement for referring patients to any person."

The authors of the rules have gone to extreme lengths here to write an exhaustive list of possible kickback schemes. They did this to make it extremely clear that any sort of consideration whatsoever for a referral is against the rules. Beyond being a violation of the rules set for the chiropractic community, receiving kickbacks is also illegal and can result in the termination of a license and potential prison time.

In addition to those potential consequences, kickbacks are also usually a bad deal for chiropractors and are rarely worth it when considering the high risk of the kickback being exposed (and the subsequent backlash and penalties).

For example, say a chiropractor gets a kickback from an attorney. The attorney, like many attorneys offering kickbacks, is involved in other immoral or illegal activities. He gets caught with a more serious criminal charge and is looking for leverage. He then offers the authorities information about the kickbacks in exchange for a more lenient sentence. Instead of looking at five years in prison, he's going to spend one year in jail because he ratted on the chiropractor and exposed the kickback operation.

This is the most common way that kickback schemes are exposed, and it is a relatively frequent occurrence. It happens every year or two, when a bunch of chiropractors, lawyers, and MDs get busted for a large-scale kickback scheme. The high risk of exposure and astronomically higher consequences make kickbacks a foolish endeavor, in addition to being an immoral one.

It's worth noting that Doctors of Chiropractic can get involved in kickback situations accidentally. By way of example, I had a chiropractor email me and ask the following question: "I have been sending my patients to an online vitamin shop for years. I think they sell a quality product. Recently, that shop reached out to me and told me that for every patient that used a special promo code, the patient would get twenty percent off their order and the shop would send me a $20 coupon to use on its website. Since I was referring patients there before, is there any problem with this?"

There is absolutely a problem here. The doctor is transitioning from referring his patients somewhere in exchange for nothing to receiving a benefit for doing it. The receipt of a discount in exchange for a referral is specifically prohibited by the rules. This doctor can keep referring his patients to the site—and can even help his patients out with a code that will get *them* a discount—but he cannot accept the $20 coupons.

As a rule, if it sounds too good to be true, it usually is. If somebody is offering a chiropractor money or anything of value in exchange for sending a patient somewhere—be it an attorney, or a vitamin store, or a gym, or a medical clinic—the chiropractor should be wary and should likely steer clear of the offer.

CHAPTER 14

PERSONAL INJURY DO'S AND DON'TS

Don'ts in Personal Injury

Shawn Steel:

- **Don't miss a big injury.** Sometimes, doctors miss a major injury in a personal injury case, either because they were focusing on other things or because of simple neglect. This can happen in many different ways and can be prevented by paying close attention to the details of the case, previous medical reports, and the patient's own narrative of events, as well as the impact of the injury on the patient's life.

As an example, we once represented a professional guitarist who was on tour when his car was hit and flipped over. He got a particularly nasty series of injuries, including musculoskeletal neck and lower-back problems. He also fractured his right thumb and injured other parts of his right hand, which was a very serious injury since it meant he temporarily could not play guitar and therefore, could not work. The chiropractor in the case issued a beautifully written report about the neck and back injuries and the patient's recovery. However, he didn't include anything about the hand injury, which was in some ways the most crucial injury for the patient's personal injury case, as it massively impacted his livelihood.

We were able to compensate for that mistake however, chiropractors have to be aware that a trauma/personal injury patient usually has a number of different issues and injuries. As care providers, chiropractors are responsible for mentioning and documenting all relevant issues. This is true even if they aren't treating a certain issue and are giving the patient a referral to a specialist.

- **Don't miss the elephant in the room.** In some cases, chiropractors miss a key injury in their reports. In others, they miss something so obvious about the patient (though maybe not directly related to an accident) that it changes the dynamic of the whole case, such as a major pre-existing condition.

One example from my practice is a patient we met in person for the first time at the deposition. The chiropractor who referred her to us noted in the report that the patient was in a car accident and had neck pain. When we met with her, we were surprised to see she was in a wheelchair, and in fact, she was a quadriplegic with very limited use of her hands. The patient had her car set up in such a way that she was able to legally drive with special mechanisms designed for quadriplegics.

Now, this client's accident had nothing to do with her status as a quadriplegic. She was rear-ended with no way to protect herself, even if she weren't a quadriplegic. However, the fact that she was a wheelchair-dependent quadriplegic was an "elephant in the room" in this case. The chiropractor may have thought it was considerate not to mention her condition, but a fact like that can be pivotal for the patient in a personal injury context. When arguing with the insurance company about compensation and settlements, I would focus less on her microinjuries and more on the fact that her injuries from the accident had had a much greater negative impact on her life than they would have had were she not wheelchair bound.

By way of another example, if a patient is a cancer survivor, chiropractors should feature that in their reports. Being a cancer survivor may impact recovery in specific ways, depending on the physical impact cancer had on the patient's body. There is a great fear among cancer survivors that a situation (especially an injury or trauma) will result in the return of their cancer. These anxieties trouble patients and trouble recovery, as well. Many times, doctors don't talk about these pre-existing injuries because they're not interviewing patients adequately about their history. Others leave them out because they fear the insurance company might be able to use the pre-existing condition to get out of paying for the impacts of the injury. Leaving out a pre-existing condition from a chiropractor's report generally does not help a personal injury case, and it can do quite a bit of damage to a case. Chiropractors should assume that the defense will find out about all pre-existing conditions and that when it does, it will question the decision to leave them out of a report. Whether it was through ignorance or, worse, intentional deception, the defense will use the omission against the chiropractor and the patient.

Therefore, we urge chiropractors not to avoid discussing pre-existing conditions. They are often vitally important to the diagnosis and to the understanding of what the patient's going through. In fact, when we learn of a patient's pre-existing condition, we suggest a consultation with doctors who treated the patient for the condition or a request for the notes of the doctors in the case. For instance, if a patient has a pre-existing case of fibromyalgia, the chiropractor may want to talk to the patient's rheumatologist or any of the other doctors and specialists who have been treating the patient over the years. Pull those records.

- **Don't fail to disclose the care history with the patient.** As we mentioned previously in this book, many patients are loyal to chiropractors for many years, a loyalty that often extends to their children and even grandchildren. It is not uncommon for a chiropractor to treat a regular patient for a new personal injury–related condition. If a person has been a patient before a traumatic injury, the person will likely come to the same chiropractor for treatment after a traumatic injury.

Chiropractors should always disclose if they have treated a patient before. If they don't, insurance companies usually find out and become suspicious.

It is standard practice for insurance companies to check the patient's medical treatment history, and if they find that the claimant was a patient of the chiropractor before the latest injury occurred, they will at the very least raise a red flag. It is much better to plainly state that the client has been a patient of the practice for however many years before the accident and to state the reason the patient was being seen before the recent injury.

Do's in Personal Injury

Alexander C. Eisner:

- **Do create a home care program.** It is vital to create a home care program for the patient to follow through on after leaving the office. This is an essential component of recovery and care. A home care program can look different depending on the patient but can include elements such as exercises, activities to avoid, and other adjustments that can be made in daily life to help with healing. This is important for the efficacy of treatment, which impacts both for the health of the patient and the chiropractor's ability to get paid. If insurance companies see the treatment includes no home care program, they may be able to resist paying the bills in full and on time.

Shawn Steel: Home exercise is essential for patients.

1. Multiple videos exist with programs designed for specific injuries that make it easy for patients to follow along.
2. Patients respect their chiropractor's integrity and are made to take responsibility for their own healing by including unbilled home care *with* chiropractic treatment.
3. Chiropractors need to regularly examine patients to establish their level of compliance and refresh the program.

Alexander C. Eisner:

- **Do recruit a triage team.** As we mentioned previously, it is important to gather a network of referral doctors and medical professionals who are pro-chiropractic, ethical, and well regarded. They could include orthopedists, pain management specialists, neurosurgeons, physical therapists, acupuncturists, and a number of other types of medical service providers. Having a small group of doctors and medical professionals who are trustworthy and able to deal with trauma is vital to any healthy personal injury practice, especially from a chiropractor's point of view.

Shawn Steel: It is essential to remember that from time to time, every chiropractor is going to need a medical specialist that deals with severe trauma issues outside of their scope of practice. Don't wait for patients to find their own doctor or specialist. For one thing, some doctors and specialists are viciously anti-chiropractic and may impact the chiropractor's relationship with the patient. In addition, being able to provide reliable references for a patient makes the patient feel well cared for and bolsters the chiropractor's reputation and trustworthiness.

Alexander C. Eisner:

- **Do bill personal injury patients monthly.** It is important to bill personal injury clients monthly (even if payment is not due every month). It is important that patients understand how billing works, how much their bill increases each month, and exactly what they are being charged for.

This is especially important if patients are being billed on lien. It's essential to be clear with them that the practice is putting the costs of their treatment on hold but that the costs are increasing with every visit and that the costs are expected to be paid out of the proceeds of the personal injury case. Even if a client initially understands this, it can be easy to forget or lose sight of it.

Keeping the client in the loop when it comes to billing avoids unnecessary sticker shock, confusion, and other issues that arise, which may lead clients to allege that they are being overcharged or falsely charged. It also gives clients some buy-in to the charging and treatment process. We have found that when the time comes for settlement and some medical bills are being reduced, informed clients are more likely to advocate for a chiropractor through their attorneys. If clients understand exactly why a certain amount was billed, they are more likely to ask their attorneys not to cut the bill.

- **Do take cash for MIST cases.** MIST cases are cases that involve minor impact, soft tissue injuries. It is a derogatory pneumonic used by insurance companies to describe cases for which they intend to offer no money or coverage. When used by insurance companies, the acronym MIST refers to cases in which the insurance company is claiming that no injuries were really sustained.

Chiropractors know that there are many types of invisible injuries and that even minor injuries deserve treatment. However, from a compensation and payment angle, they should consider the viability of a patient's personal injury case when considering how to seek payment.

Shawn Steel: Let's say the chiropractor has a patient who was in a minor car accident. If the patient shows the chiropractor a picture of the accident and the damage is difficult to spot, or if the chiropractor asks about the pain level and the patient says it's a 2 or 3 out of 10 on the pain scale, the case is likely to be considered a MIST case by the insurance company. This means the insurance company is very unlikely to offer coverage and compensation and that the chiropractor should not offer payment on a lien if the intention is to get paid in full (or at all). Rather, chiropractors should accept cash payments from these types of clients. Everyone deserves care, but chiropractors shouldn't have to run themselves into the ground by operating involuntarily free clinics.

CHAPTER 15

HIRING A PERSONAL INJURY LITIGATION ATTORNEY

Alexander C. Eisner: Patients are often hesitant to seek the assistance of an attorney after an accident. Sometimes they are concerned about the stigma associated with bad attorneys or fraudulent personal injury claims or sometimes they believe they can handle negotiations with the insurance company themselves. Regardless, getting a personal injury case into the hands of a good, pro-chiropractic attorney is one of the best things chiropractors can do to protect their liens and get paid.

I often use a formulation by friend and well-known chiropractor Dr. Brad Glowaki. He calls it the "Mavin Mousetrap." He tells patients who have been in accidents caused by another driver that although not every case is right for an attorney, and he certainly doesn't want patients to have to go through the whole litigation process if it's not right for them, he believes they should contact an attorney if one of three things happens:

- If the insurance company of the person who hit the patient contacts the patient and wants to record a statement.
- If the insurance company wants the patient to sign something.
- If the insurance company sends someone to the patient's home to talk to the patient.

I have added an additional condition to this list, which is:

- If the insurance company tells the patient that hiring an attorney will likely decrease the amount of money the patient will get.

Dr. Glowaki reminds his patients of the truth, which is that insurance companies may be friendly at first but that they are not acting on behalf of the patient. The things they are doing are not things done to protect the patient; they are things done to protect the insurance company.

The beauty of these standards is that third-party insurance companies almost always do one of these things. When they do, and the patient comes to the chiropractor and says, "Oh my God, they did the thing that you told me about," the chiropractor can tell the patient that it's time to get an attorney to protect the patient's rights and interests. This tactic is fairly effective in making the idea to see an attorney the patient's idea. It is especially effective when paired with smart referrals to high-quality, pro-chiropractic attorneys who can be trusted to pay a bill when the case is over (if the chiropractor doesn't know any such attorneys, we'd be happy to point them in the right direction *wink*).

What Factors Should a Treating Doctor Consider When Trying to Get Paid for a Personal Injury Case?

Alexander C. Eisner: The first question to consider is whether or not there *is* a personal injury case. The answer depends on the viability of the case and then, obviously, if there is money available with which one can be paid.

The second question is how much money is available. This usually boils down to insurance policies and limits, unless an attorney is truly out for blood and willing to go after a defendant's house, car, or other personal belongings (which seldom happens). When considering available insurance money, we're usually considering third-party policies (i.e., the policies of the person who caused the accident). How much money does that person have in a policy? We may also be considering the patient's insurance, including whether the patient has underinsured/uninsured motorist coverage (and if so, how much).

There are certainly additional considerations, such as if there is a government entity or a corporation partly or entirely responsible for the accident. These can represent additional recovery sources. However, for the most part, we're just looking at policy limits of the third party and policy limits of the first party. This information should be obtained as quickly as possible so that the chiropractor doesn't accidentally put too much money on a lien.

Chiropractors sometimes claim that a patient is too injured to allow for treatment on a lien, as the amount of treatment the patient needs exceeds the amount that the lien will allow. However, this is not necessarily an issue. In these cases, treatment doesn't need to be put exclusively on the lien. Certainly, chiropractors can bill on a lien up to a certain point, and then if the case can't support payment on the lien any more, they can transition that patient into a cash patient. With liens, the name of the game is making sure that, at the end of the case, the chiropractor can reasonably request that the lien be paid in full.

If a Patient Has MedPay, How Can Chiropractors Make Sure They Receive Payments from MedPay?

Shawn Steel: MedPay/PIP is the gold standard for personal injury. The chiropractor gets paid without waiting for the case to settle, get litigated, or go through final resolution by the attorney. The problem with MedPay is that all too often, particularly in California, attorneys like to "intercept" (read: steal) the MedPay funds that are supposed to go to the chiropractor, putting them into their own pockets and their own trust accounts. Some of these attorneys steal the entire sum, while others simply take a third of it (see Chapters 8 and 9).

Intercepting MedPay payments is an objective anti-chiropractic act and a firing offense. As soon as there is an indication that an attorney is doing this, the chiropractor should talk to the patient about it and explain why what their attorney is doing is unethical and wrong. It is impossible to negotiate with attorneys who have made a conscious decision to take MedPay payments that don't belong to them. Most of the attorneys that I know are ethical, hard-working, and honest; they do not ever take MedPay payments. They consider that shallow, embarrassing, and rapacious. Attorneys that do this are not to be reasoned with; they rather should be fired and replaced with someone more ethical and competent.

How Do Policy Limits and Billing Affect the Odds That Chiropractors Will Get Paid?

Shawn Steel: A chiropractor should always have an honest discussion with a patient and, ideally, the patient's attorney regarding policy limits. The patient might have a serious injury with multiple fractures, but if the defendant only has $15,000 in insurance, the case will likely involve a lot of care for which the chiropractor may not get full compensation. Chiropractors can decide to take cases like that, but they need to know all the information about them up front.

Chiropractors might be considering taking on a case with serious injuries but not know anything about the insurance policies involved. This is why it's essential to talk to the personal injury attorney. If the patient needs and deserves a lot of care and the chiropractor provides minimal care because they are not certain that they will be compensated, the chiropractor is doing a disservice to the patient. To avoid this, the **chiropractor needs to be working in collaboration with the personal injury attorney.**

When an insurance company gets a chiropractic bill and report, it doesn't look at the report first; it looks at the bill first. One of the first steps it takes is to look at the size of the bill and then divide it by the number of visits. That's what's known as the **average daily fee (ADF).** An ADF includes what's called "front-loading." This means it includes the costs of the initial evaluation, x-rays and other images, and multiple modalities at the start of treatment. That's an expensive day. By the fifth visit or tenth visit, the bill for each visit should be much less than that initial visit.

For example, if the bill is $3,000 for thirty visits, the ADF is $100. Most insurance companies are going to consider that reasonable and necessary. This means that the charges for individual visits have been kept relatively low so that the ADF stays low. However, if the ADF includes $200 or $300 a visit, then insurance companies are going to push back. This can involve denials, delays, and refusals of payment and requests for depositions to explain pricing. It may even include blacklisting. While some chiropractors will tout the time they got away with billing $200+ per visit, that is certainly the exception, not the rule.

Personal injury pays more than any other insurance consideration presently, and many insurance companies readily reimburse for "reasonable" ADFs. The American Automobile Association has told me numerous times that it considers a reasonable ADF to be around $125 and will happily pay it. This is much more than Medicare, Blue Cross, or worker's compensation is willing to pay.

It's like leading a wagon train. The best place to be is in the middle; it's much safer there than in the front, and chiropractors are much less vulnerable to undercharging there than those at the back.

Alexander C. Eisner: What?

CHAPTER 16

WHAT HAPPENS WHEN A PATIENT HIRES AN ANTI-CHIROPRACTIC ATTORNEY

Alexander C. Eisner: When a patient fires an attorney and the chiropractor had a lien with that attorney, the lien agreement with that attorney is no longer good in most jurisdictions. A lien is just a contract. The chiropractor should always have the patient and the attorney sign it. That way, if a patient fires an attorney, the chiropractor still has a valid contract, since the patient is also on the lien.

If a patient fires an attorney and hires a new one, the chiropractor's first order of business is to send the lien over and ask the new attorney to sign it. If the attorney refuses, the chiropractor is going to want to have a conversation with the patient about how the new attorney is setting up an uncomfortable situation by not signing the lien. At that point, the chiropractor can tell the patient that a conversion to cash payment will have to take place unless the patient can get the attorney to sign the lien or fire the attorney and hire one who will sign the lien. Make sure you explain to your patient that that lien is your only protection against getting stiffed.

Once an attorney signs the new lien, all the billing is covered as it was with the previous attorney. The reason why it's important to have an attorney on the lien is that an attorney has ethical responsibilities (legally known as fiduciary duties) and also has a law firm and a license to contend with if the attorney were to get sued for breaching a chiropractic lien. In contrast, an individual client can skip out on a lien, and it can then be very difficult to collect money from that person. Chiropractors never want to be in the situation of pursuing, or suing, patients so they can collect money from them.

How Soon Should Chiropractors Get Paid After a Case Closes?

Shawn Steel: Chiropractors should get paid no later than sixty days after a personal injury case closes unless there are some extraordinary circumstances that make this impossible. However, all too often, chiropractors wait far longer than that. Sometimes, they never get paid on their lien at all. Other times, they get a letter from the attorney saying, "Look, I know your bill is $3,000, but I'm paying you $750 because we've had problems," or worse, sometimes they'll just get a check in the mail for $750 with no explanation.

Chiropractors need to learn to defend themselves against this sort of treatment. We have a three-step letter for collecting money from dishonest attorneys (see Appendix B: Personal Injury Lien Collection Kit). If an attorney refuses to pay what is lawfully and ethically owed, the chiropractor can send the attorney a letter (certified mail) with a deadline for payment and tell the attorney two things: (1) If the attorney doesn't pay what is owed by a certain date, the chiropractor will file a complaint with the State Bar. This is a big deal for the attorney and costs the chiropractor nothing. (2) The chiropractor is going to sue the attorney. Most chiropractic bills are under $10,000, so this suit will likely take place in a small claims court in most jurisdictions. This sort of letter has worked for dozens of doctors for over twenty years in California with a very high rate of success.

If the attorney receives the letter and the deadline passes without payment, we usually recommend waiting three to five days and then filing a lawsuit in small claims court. This type of filing is fast and easy. I think every chiropractor should do it at least once to find out how easy it is. Almost every chiropractor we have helped through the process remarks on feeling vindicated when the suit is over, and they are almost always shocked at how simple the whole thing is.

Once attorneys see that chiropractors are taking action, the vast majority who did not respond to the letter will respond to the lawsuit. Is the chiropractor probably going to burn a bridge with that attorney? Absolutely. But the chiropractor will earn a reputation for expecting to be paid for billed services (and the chiropractor wouldn't have wanted to work with that scummy attorney anyway). This boils down to self-worth, and ultimately, chiropractors are only worth what they demand payment for.

CHAPTER 17

COMMON LIES BAD ATTORNEYS TELL

Alexander C. Eisner: Here are some common lies we hear from anti-chiropractic attorneys.

- **"Chiropractic won't help a personal injury case."** Of course it will! Chiropractic treatment helps a personal injury case in a plethora of ways of which chiropractors are already aware, including treating patients for injuries, helping them get a non-surgical, non-narcotic treatment for pain, and giving the personal injury case a quarterback.

- **"Only attorneys can collect MedPay."** This is also obviously a lie. In fact, attorneys should never collect the chiropractor's MedPay payments because they are strictly intended for medical providers.
- **"Only attorneys should make referrals."** This lie is so absurd that it is borderline illegal. It advocates what is called attorney-directed treatment, which is harmful to patients. Attorneys are not medical professionals, as much as they sometimes think they are. They are not allowed to make referrals to specialists. They can assist clients in finding a referral and tell clients about doctors and medical practitioners that fit specific needs. They can even help with booking an appointment or making suggestions to the chiropractor. However, they cannot make referrals and should not try to engage in attorney-directed treatment.

- **"We tried to contact the chiropractor regarding the fee because the case settled, but the chiropractor didn't get back to us, so we gave the money to the client to pay the chiropractor."** First of all, there's no way an attorney's letter can get "lost in the mail," so if the chiropractor didn't receive it, the attorney didn't send it. Attorneys have a legal obligation to make sure chiropractors get any notice regarding the settlement of a case. In addition, the lien agreement signed by the chiropractor and the attorney is a binding legal contract, legal in all fifty states, and the attorney is in violation of that contract and likely of attorney ethics rules if they do not hold the doctor's money in trust for them.

In addition, even if the attorney really did give the money to the patient, the patient likely had no understanding at all that the money was supposed to be used to pay the chiropractor. If an attorney uses this line, it can be grounds for State Bar complaints and even lawsuits. The bottom line is, if the attorney signed the lien, the attorney is obligated to pay the chiropractor directly. The attorney cannot simply offload that responsibility to the client; to do so puts the attorney in breach of contract (in CA and in most other states).

- **"The lien is no longer valid because we transferred the case to a different attorney within our firm."** This is another obvious lie because transferring a lien within a law firm keeps the lien intact.
- **"The client told me not to pay the chiropractor."** I hear this exact excuse or some variation all too often. Variations include lines such as the client told the attorney that he or she didn't go to all those treatment sessions, or that the chiropractor is exaggerating the bill, or that the chiropractor is double-billing, or that the chiropractor hurt the client. These are all a common thread of lies that attorneys tell chiropractors, and they don't get the attorney out of his or her obligation to pay the chiropractor under the terms of the lien

(chiropractors are likely starting to see how important it is to have an attorney sign that damn lien).

- **"A third, a third, a third."** This is a lie some attorneys tell clients at the beginning of the case. They tell them that no matter what the settlement is, the attorney will get a third, the client will get a third, and all the medical practitioners (including doctors, ambulance companies, ER doctors, and specialists such as chiropractors) will share a third. This almost always means an automatic and drastic discounting of the bills of all the medical practitioners, including (and sometimes especially) the chiropractor. This is in direct opposition to what is stated in any lien.

Shawn Steel: I believe that one of the responsibilities of a personal injury attorney is to see that medical bills and chiropractic bills are handled in an ethical manner and that one of the attorney's primary goals should be to ensure that health care providers get fully compensated, so the patient doesn't get harassed by medical professionals or collection agencies. Patients need to know that. We tell our clients all the time, "Look, you're getting the best care on Earth. Nowhere else in the world will you get this high level of care for your trauma. But you need to understand that the medical practitioners are waiting for their bills to get paid, and we don't engage in reducing their bills unnecessarily." This is something that our patients understand, and we tell them straight up that if they're uncomfortable with that policy, they might want to seek the services of another attorney. I think that ought to be the gold standard for attorneys when they're doing personal injury.

Alexander C. Eisner: Chiropractic treatment is special. It's unlike any other type of treatment that a trauma victim is likely to receive, and it should be treated as sacrosanct in the personal injury world. The reason why our practice relies heavily on chiropractic referral is no secret. It's simply based on paying the chiropractors what we believe they're worth, which is one hundred percent of their bills. The reason no other attorneys can replicate what we're doing in the chiropractic community is that they're simply not willing to treat chiropractors the way they deserve to be treated and make a commitment to honor their bills as often as possible.

Shawn Steel: There is a reason why a huge number of people in America, when they have a car accident, see a chiropractor rather than their primary care physician, an orthopedist, or any other type of doctor. I think attorneys are smart to work with, cooperate with, and support chiropractic and chiropractors, and that's why we wrote this book. We want chiropractors to feel appreciated, supported, and capable of getting paid for their hard work.

CHAPTER 18

THE SKUNK TEST

Shawn Steel: Chiropractors should carefully vet personal injury attorneys to figure out the likelihood that the attorney will treat them fairly. We have four questions that chiropractors can use to assess attorneys when first reaching out. The answers give chiropractors lots of useful information about attorneys and whether or not they will be fair business partners. The questions should be answered on a pass/fail basis, and we do not recommend working with attorneys that fail any one of the four.

1. **Will the attorney sign the chiropractor's lien (with no modifications)?** This is a very simple question. If an attorney says yes and promptly returns a signed, unmodified lien, the attorney has passed this test. If the attorney attempts to modify the lien, thank them! They have just showed you exactly how they intend to screw you when the case settles. They have failed this test.
2. **Has the attorney fully disclosed all insurance information?** Ask the attorney for a full breakdown of all the insurance information. Attorneys always know as much as there is to know about available insurance funds at any given point in a case. If an attorney is hesitant or reluctant to give a chiropractor any insurance information, or simply won't cooperate with the chiropractor, the attorney has failed this test. If the attorney fully and readily discloses all insurance information and is happy to answer any questions about it, the attorney has passed.

3. **Will the attorney call and discuss the case with the chiropractor?** Ask the attorney if, in a quick call, the details of the case could be outlined. This doesn't have to involve a long, formal, or even in-person meeting. However, any good attorney should be able to give the chiropractor at least five to ten minutes of time. In the call, ask the attorney basic questions about the case. Ask what the potential value of the case is from the attorney's point of view, as well as the potential liabilities of the case. Ask about the chiropractor's level of risk. Consider asking point-blank, "If I treat and bill reasonably in this case, can I expect to get paid in full?" If the attorney takes the call from the chiropractor in a timely manner and discusses the case openly and respectfully, the attorney passes the test.
4. **What is the attorney's attitude toward chiropractic?** If speaking with the attorney directly, ask a few questions designed to ferret out the attorney's opinions about chiropractic. Ask if the attorney or a loved one has ever been

to a chiropractor and had a positive outcome. If the attorney says no, all hope is not lost. Ask if the attorney would like to come down to the chiropractic practice, see what the chiropractor does, and get a free adjustment. One can tell a lot about an attorney based on how the attorney feels about chiropractors and chiropractic. If the attorney doesn't believe in what the chiropractor is doing or, worse, is openly hostile toward chiropractic, the attorney is broadcasting how the chiropractor's bill will be treated when the case resolves, and there is probably going to be a bad result with that attorney.

If a patient has engaged an attorney who does not pass these tests, the chiropractor can tell the patient exactly what is happening. For instance, the chiropractor can say, "Look, this attorney isn't signing the lien or communicating with me, so I do not feel comfortable working with this person. Would you like a reference to one of the attorneys I frequently work with?" If the patient then goes out and fires that attorney and gets a better one, that will ultimately help the patient and also help the chiropractor.

Alexander C. Eisner: Remember that by virtue of the fact that you are actively making your patients feel better each time you see them, you have infinitely more credibility in their eyes than their attorney will ever hope to have. Use this. Ask your patient if they believe you should be paid for the work you are doing for them. Ask them if they think it's right that you should risk a huge loss on their personal injury case. Ask them to be you advocate with their attorney and remember that a client is free to fire their attorney at will and hire a new one for any reason at any time. Bottom line, you should not have to be beholden to an attorney that you know is going to screw you when the case resolves.

EPILOGUE

Alexander C. Eisner: One thing Shawn and I have learned through our years of lecturing and working in the personal injury sphere is that personal injury practice can be incredibly rewarding for the astute chiropractor, but most Doctors of Chiropractic come out of college without the tools to succeed. Because of this, many chiropractors' first few experiences with personal injury are awful, and they simply write off the whole of personal injury as "not worth the hassle." In personal injury, just like in life, it boils down to how well you play the game and what level of respect you demand while playing it. The longer you play, the better at it you will become and the more rewarding it will ultimately be. This, however, relies on your willingness to stand your ground (and ask for help when you get stuck). Chiropractors are some of the most dedicated health care practitioners with whom I have ever had the pleasure of working. They didn't get into chiropractic for the money or the glory or the social standing most of the time; they got into it to help heal people. This being the case, there are few people more in need of your skillset and caring than those who have just experienced a traumatic musculoskeletal injury. These people need you and, in the absence of good chiropractors, would otherwise be pouring into medical doctor's offices and then pharmacies all over the globe. Your calling is healing these people without scalpels, needles, or drugs and advocating for them throughout the entire healing process, regardless of who else you have to enlist to get the job done. The pairing of a good chiropractor and a good attorney can change the lives of people who really need us. So keep your head up, get out there, and fight the good fight (and try and have a good time while you're at it).

Shawn Steel: I have dedicated my life to serving trauma victims, just like many of you have. It is awful to see the ways in which many chiropractors are treated for committing the "crime" of attempting to aid their patients. I have always said that with the right tools, any chiropractor can be a great personal injury chiropractor. My calling is and has always been to give chiropractors those tools in the ever-evolving personal injury landscape, and this book represents over forty years of wisdom that I have had the pleasure of imparting to chiropractors. I hope that this book serves as yet another tool in your arsenal to aid in your practice of good chiropractic for your personal injury patients.

APPENDIX A: SAM COLLINS'S TOP 200 TRAUMA CODES

PI Trauma Related Diagnosis (Head and Spine)
www.hjrosscompany.com

ICD10	Code Description
	Headaches
G44.309	Post-traumatic headache, unspecified
G44.319	Acute post-traumatic headache
G44.329	Chronic post-traumatic headache
G44.86	Cervicogenic headache
	Concussion, Dizziness, Vertigo
S06.0X0A	Concussion without loss of consciousness, initial encounter
F07.81	Post concussion syndrome (postconucssional syndrome)
H81.4	Vertigo
R42	Dizziness and lightheadedness
	TMJ
S03.41XA	Sprain of jaw, right side, initial encounter
S03.42XA	Sprain of jaw,left side, initial encounter
S03.43XA	Sprain of jaw, bilateral , initial encounter
M26.601	Right temporomandibular (TMJ)joint disorder, unspecified
M26.602	Left temporomandibular (TMJ)joint disorder, unspecified
M26.603	Bilateral temporomandibular (TMJ)joint disorder, unspecified
M79.11	Myalgia, muscle of mastication
	Sprain and Strain
	Cervical Spine
S13.4XXA	Sprain of ligaments of cervical spine initial encounter (active treatment)
S13.8XXA	Sprain of joints and ligaments of other parts of neck initial encounter (lower cervical)
S13.0XXA	Traumatic rupture of cervical intervertebral disc, initial encounter
S16.1XXA	Strain of muscle, fascia and tendon at neck level initial encounter (active treatment)
S14.2XXA	Injury of nerve root of cervical spine, initial encounter
S14.3XXA	Injury of brachial plexus, initial encounter
	Thoracic Spine
S23.3XXA	Sprain of ligaments of thoracic spine initial encounter (active treatment)
S29.012A	Strain of muscle and tendon of back wall of thorax initial encounter (active treatment)
S24.2XXA	Injury of nerve root of thoracic spine, initial encounter
S23.0XXA	Traumatic rupture of thoracic intervertebral disc, initial encounter
	Lumbosacral Spine
S33.5XXA	Sprain of ligaments of lumbar spine, initial encounter (active treatment)
S33.5XXS	Sprain of ligaments of lumbar spine, sequelae
S39.012A	Strain of muscle, fascia and tendon of lower back, initial encounter (active treatment)
S39.012S	Strain of muscle, fascia and tendon of lower back, sequelae
S33.8XXA	Sprain of other parts of lumbar spine and pelvis, initial encounter (active treatment)
S33.8XXS	Sprain of other parts of lumbar spine and pelvis, sequelae
S34.21XA	Injury of nerve root of lumbar spine, initial encounter
S34.22XA	Injury of nerve root of sacral spine, initial encounter
S34.4XXA	Injury of lumbosacral plexus, initial encounter
S33.0XXA	Traumatic rupture of lumbar intervertebral disc, initial encounter
S74.01XA	Injury of sciatic nerve at hip and thigh level, right leg, initial encounter
S74.02XA	Injury of sciatic nerve at hip and thigh level, left leg, initial encounter

	Nerve & Radiculopathy
	Cervical
M53.0	Cervicocranial syndrome
M53.1	Cervicobrachial syndrome
M54.11	Radiculopathy occipito-atlanto-axial region
M54.12	Radiculopathy cervical region
M54.13	Radiculopathy cervicothoracic region
G54.0	Brachial plexus disorders
G54.2	Cervical root disorders, not elsewhere classified
	Thoracic
M54.14	Radiculopathy thoracic (neuritis)
M54.15	Radiculopathy thoracolumbar
G54.0	Brachial plexus lesions (thoracic outlet syndrome)
G54.3	Thoracic root disorders, not elsewhere classified
G58.0	Intercostal Neuropathy
	Lumbosacral
M54.16	Radiculopathy, lumbar region
M54.17	Radiculopathy, lumbosacral region
M54.18	Radiculopathy, sacrococcygeal region
M54.31	Sciatica, right side
M54.32	Sciatica, left side
M54.41	Lumbago with sciatica, right side
M54.42	Lumbago with sciatica, left side
G54.1	Lumbosacral plexus disorders
G54.4	Lumbosacral root disorders, not elsewhere classified
G57.01	Lesion of sciatic nerve, right lower limb (piriformis syndrome)
G57.02	Lesion of sciatic nerve, left lower limb (piriformis syndrome)
G57.03	Lesion of sciatic nerve, bilateral lower limb (piriformis syndrome)
	Disc (Type 1 exclude- do not code spinal pain codes M54 codes with disc diagnosis)
	Cervical
M50.01	Cervical disc disorder with myelopathy high cervical (C2-3 C3-4)
M50.021	Cervical disc disorder at C4-C5 level with myelopathy
M50.022	Cervical disc disorder at C5-C6 level with myelopathy
M50.023	Cervical disc disorder at C6-C7 level with myelopathy
M50.11	Cervical disc disorder with radiculopathy high cervical (C2-3 C3-4)
M50.121	Cervical disc disorder at C4-C5 level with radiculopathy
M50.122	Cervical disc disorder at C5-C6 level with radiculopathy
M50.123	Cervical disc disorder at C6-C7 level with radiculopathy
M50.13	Cervical disc disorder with radiculopathy, cervicothoracic region
M50.21	Cervical disc displacement C2-3, C3-4 region
M50.221	Other cervical disc displacement at C4-C5 level
M50.222	Other cervical disc displacement at C5-C6 level
M50.223	Other cervical disc displacement at C6-C7 level
M50.23	Cervical disc displacement C7-T1 region
M50.30	Cervical disc degeneration, unspecified cervical region
M50.31	Cervical disc degeneration high cervical C2-3 C3-4
M50.321	Other cervical disc degeneration at C4-C5 level

M50.322	Other cervical disc degeneration at C5-C6 level
M50.323	Other cervical disc degeneration at C6-C7 level
M50.33	Cervical disc degeneration cervicothoracic region C7-T1
M50.81	Other cervical disc disorders, high cervical region (C2-3 C3-4)
M50.820	Other cervical disc disorders, mid-cervical region, unspecified level
M50.821	Other cervical disc disorders at C4-C5 level
M50.822	Other cervical disc disorders at C5-C6 level
M50.823	Other cervical disc disorders at C6-C7 level
M50.83	Other cervical disc disorders, cervicothoracic region
M50.90	Cervical disc disorder, unspecified cervical region
M50.91	Cervical disc disorder, unspecified high cervical (C2-3 C3-4)
M50.920	Unspecified cervical disc disorder, mid-cervical, unspecified level
M50.921	Unspecified cervical disc disorder at C4-C5 level
M50.922	Unspecified cervical disc disorder at C5-C6 level
M50.921	Unspecified cervical disc disorder at C4-C5 level
M50.922	Unspecified cervical disc disorder at C5-C6 level
M50.923	Unspecified cervical disc disorder at C6-C7 level
M50.93	Cervical disc disorder, unspecified, cervicothoracic C7-T1 region
	Thoracic
M51.04	Intervertebral disc disorders with myelopathy, thoracic region
M51.05	Intervertebral disc disorders with myelopathy, thoracolumbar region
M51.14	Intervertebral disc disorders with radiculopathy, thoracic region
M51.15	Intervertebral disc disorders with radiculopathy, thoracolumbar region
M51.24	Thoracic intervertebral disc displacement
M51.34	Thoracic intervertebral disc degeneration
M51.35	Thoracolumbar intervertebral disc degeneration
M51.84	Other intervertebral disc disorders, thoracic region
M51.85	Other intervertebral disc disorders, thoracolumbar region
M51.9	Unspecified thoracic, thoracolumbar and lumbosacral intervertebral disc disorder
	Lumbosacral
M51.06	Intervertebral disc disorders with myelopathy, lumbar region
M51.16	Intervertebral disc disorders with radiculopathy, lumbar region
M51.17	Intervertebral disc disorders with radiculopathy, lumbosacral region
M51.26	Intervertebral disc displacement, lumbar region
M51.27	Intervertebral disc displacement, lumbosacral region
M51.36	Lumbar intervertebral disc degeneration
M51.37	Lumbosacral intervertebral disc degeneration
M51.86	Other intervertebral disc disorders, lumbar region
M51.87	Other intervertebral disc disorders, lumbosacral region
M51.9	Unspecified thoracic, thoracolumbar and lumbosacral intervertebral disc disorder
	Other Pain or Conditions (facet, musculoskeletal disorder etc.)
M53.81	Other specified dorsopathies, occipito-atlanto-axial region
M53.82	Other specified dorsopathies, cervical region
M53.83	Other specified dorsopathies, cervicothoracic region
M53.84	Other specified dorsopathies, thoracic region
M53.85	Other specified dorsopathies, thoracolumbar region
M53.86	Other specified dorsopathies, lumbar region

M50.322	Other cervical disc degeneration at C5-C6 level
M50.323	Other cervical disc degeneration at C6-C7 level
M50.33	Cervical disc degeneration cervicothoracic region C7-T1
M50.81	Other cervical disc disorders, high cervical region (C2-3 C3-4)
M50.820	Other cervical disc disorders, mid-cervical region, unspecified level
M50.821	Other cervical disc disorders at C4-C5 level
M50.822	Other cervical disc disorders at C5-C6 level
M50.823	Other cervical disc disorders at C6-C7 level
M50.83	Other cervical disc disorders, cervicothoracic region
M50.90	Cervical disc disorder, unspecified cervical region
M50.91	Cervical disc disorder, unspecified high cervical (C2-3 C3-4)
M50.920	Unspecified cervical disc disorder, mid-cervical, unspecified level
M50.921	Unspecified cervical disc disorder at C4-C5 level
M50.922	Unspecified cervical disc disorder at C5-C6 level
M50.921	Unspecified cervical disc disorder at C4-C5 level
M50.922	Unspecified cervical disc disorder at C5-C6 level
M50.923	Unspecified cervical disc disorder at C6-C7 level
M50.93	Cervical disc disorder, unspecified, cervicothoracic C7-T1 region
	Thoracic
M51.04	Intervertebral disc disorders with myelopathy, thoracic region
M51.05	Intervertebral disc disorders with myelopathy, thoracolumbar region
M51.14	Intervertebral disc disorders with radiculopathy, thoracic region
M51.15	Intervertebral disc disorders with radiculopathy, thoracolumbar region
M51.24	Thoracic intervertebral disc displacement
M51.34	Thoracic intervertebral disc degeneration
M51.35	Thoracolumbar intervertebral disc degeneration
M51.84	Other intervertebral disc disorders, thoracic region
M51.85	Other intervertebral disc disorders, thoracolumbar region
M51.9	Unspecified thoracic, thoracolumbar and lumbosacral intervertebral disc disorder
	Lumbosacral
M51.06	Intervertebral disc disorders with myelopathy, lumbar region
M51.16	Intervertebral disc disorders with radiculopathy, lumbar region
M51.17	Intervertebral disc disorders with radiculopathy, lumbosacral region
M51.26	Intervertebral disc displacement, lumbar region
M51.27	Intervertebral disc displacement, lumbosacral region
M51.36	Lumbar intervertebral disc degeneration
M51.37	Lumbosacral intervertebral disc degeneration
M51.86	Other intervertebral disc disorders, lumbar region
M51.87	Other intervertebral disc disorders, lumbosacral region
M51.9	Unspecified thoracic, thoracolumbar and lumbosacral intervertebral disc disorder
	Other Pain or Conditions (facet, musculoskeletal disorder etc.)
M53.81	Other specified dorsopathies, occipito-atlanto-axial region
M53.82	Other specified dorsopathies, cervical region
M53.83	Other specified dorsopathies, cervicothoracic region
M53.84	Other specified dorsopathies, thoracic region
M53.85	Other specified dorsopathies, thoracolumbar region
M53.86	Other specified dorsopathies, lumbar region

M53.87	Other specified dorsopathies, lumbosacral region
M53.88	Other specified dorsopathies, sacral and sacrococcygeal region
M53.3	Sacrococcygeal disorders, not elsewhere classified
	Muscle
M79.10	Myalgia, unspecified site
M79.12	Myalgia of auxiliary muscles, head and neck
M79.18	Myalgia, other site
M79.7	Fibromyalgia
M60.88	Other myositis, other site
M62.830	Muscle spasm of back
M62.838	Other muscle spasm
	Spondylosis Arthritis
M47.891	Other spondylosis, occipito-atlanto-axial region
M47.892	Other spondylosis, cervical region
M47.893	Other spondylosis, cervicothoracic region
M47.894	Other spondylosis, thoracic region
M47.895	Other spondylosis, thoracolumbar region
M47.895	Other spondylosis, thoracolumbar region
M47.896	Other spondylosis, lumbar region
M47.897	Other spondylosis, lumbosacral region
M47.898	Other spondylosis, sacral and sacrococcygeal region
	Kyphosis and Lordosis
M40.03	Postural Kyphosis cervicothoracic
M40.04	Postural Kyphosis thoracic
M40.05	Postural Kyphosis thoracolumbar
M40.12	Other secondary kyphosis, cervical region
M40.13	Other secondary kyphosis, cervicothoracic region
M40.14	Other secondary kyphosis, thoracic region
M40.15	Other secondary kyphosis, thoracolumbar region
M40.292	Other kyphosis cervical
M40.293	Other kyphosis cervicothoracic region
M40.294	Other kyphosis thoracic region
M40.295	Other kyphosis thoracolumbar region
	Ligament Laxity & Spinal Instability
M24.28	Disorder of ligament, vertebrae (ligament laxity)
M53.2X1	Spinal instabilities, occipito-atlanto-axial region
M53.2X2	Spinal instabilities, cervical region
M53.2X3	Spinal instabilities, cervicothoracic region
M53.2X4	Spinal instabilities, thoracic region
M53.2X5	Spinal instabilities, thoracolumbar region
M53.2X6	Spinal instabilities, lumbar region
M53.2X7	Spinal instabilities, lumbosacral region
M53.2X8	Spinal instabilities, sacral and sacrococcygeal region
M24.28	Disorder of ligament, vertebrae (ligament laxity)

M54.9	Dorsalgia, unspecified
	Other Related Conditions
G47.00	Insomnia
R53.83	Other fatigue
R53.1	Weakness
F41.9	Anxiety disorder, unspecified
	Sequelae and Possible Residual Conditions (not listed prior)
M46.01	Spinal enthesopathy, occipito-atlanto-axial region
M46.02	Spinal enthesopathy, cervical region
M46.03	Spinal enthesopathy, cervicothoracic region
M46.04	Spinal enthesopathy, thoracic region
M46.05	Spinal enthesopathy, thoracolumbar region
M46.06	Spinal enthesopathy, lumbar region
M46.07	Spinal enthesopathy, lumbosacral region
M46.08	Spinal enthesopathy, sacral and sacrococcygeal region
M46.09	Spinal enthesopathy, multiple sites in spine
M24.50	Contracture, unspecified joint
M25.60	Stiffness of unspecified joint, not elsewhere classified, (specify spine)
M79.89	Other soft tissue disorders (swelling, inflammation)
G89.21	Chronic pain due to trauma
G89.29	Other chronic pain
G89.4	Chronic pain syndrome (Chronic pain associated with psychosocial dysfunction)

APPENDIX B: PERSONAL INJURY LIEN COLLECTION KIT

SHAWNSTEEL
LAW FIRM
PI LIEN COLLECTION KIT

One Call Only:

Don't call a PI attorney more than necessary. If they are acting in bad faith it doesn't matter how many times you call. One call we believe is sufficient to alert him or her they might have mistakenly forgot to honor your lien.

Three Easy Steps:

1. Write your Demand Letter giving the PI attorney 72 hours to pay you. This letter has collected millions for hard working doctors. Attorneys don't worry about telephone calls. But they regard written demands as something not to trifle with.

2. If the attorney does not respond, file a complaint with the State Bar. The Bar controls his license to practice. Attorneys who have a number of complaints showing they are not managing their trust account in an ethical manner will lose their license to practice. This is powerful.

3. Sue 'em if they don't pay. It might seem that Small Claims was designed for the health care provider. You can sue 2 times a year up to $10,000 if you are an individual or a sole proprietor. Corporations and other entities are limited to $5,000. In addition, a party (individuals or corporations) can file no more than two claims exceeding $2,500 in any court throughout the State of California during a calendar year.

HOWARD FIGHTBACK, DC
8383 Wilshire Boulevard #640
Beverly Hills, CA 90021

VIA CERTIFIED MAIL

John Dewey, Esq.
Dewey, Cheatum & Howe
1900 Century Blvd
Redwood, CA 95000

Re: DEMAND FOR PAYMENT IN 72 HOURS

Our Patient/Your Client	: William Victim
Date of Accident	: January 1
Amount of Lien	: $1,500.00

Dear Mr. Dewey:

Enclosed please find a copy of the medical lien signed and dated by yourself. This lien guarantees that your office will pay our office once the case is settled. We understand that the case was settled recently, and that our patient has already received compensation.

We assume that you will honor your lien contract, but your delay is causing us concern. Accordingly, we demand full and immediate payment of $1,500 (see accompanying copies of bill and report). I am sure you are familiar with the provisions of the Rules of Professional Conduct of the State Bar of California. The Bar charges you as fiduciary for monies collected in this case.

If payment is not made, we will have no alternative but to file a lawsuit against you and your firm. We prefer not to take these measures but will unless we receive the payment within 72 hours from the date of this letter.

Sincerely,

Howard Fightback, DC

CC: William Victim

Encl.: Medical lien
Medical report(s) & bill(s)
Letter from the President of the State Bar of California, Terry Anderlini

THE STATE BAR OF CALIFORNIA

555 FRANKLIN STREET
SAN FRANCISCO, CA

RECEIVED
OCT 26 1987
CALIF. CHIROPRACTIC ASSOC.

October 22, 1987

Harold Bradford
Director of Governmental Affairs
California Chiropractic Association
1700 Alhambra Boulevard, Suite 110
Sacramento, California 95816

Dear Mr. Bradford:

Thank you for your letter of October 8, 1987 and the attachments concerning the practice of some attorneys refusing to honor medical liens.

I have contacted members of the State Bar staff about your concerns and have learned that members of the State Bar of California are currently subject to discipline for failing to honor a valid lien.

In Johnstone v. State Bar (1966) 64Cal.2d 153, 155 [49 Cal.Rptr. 97], the attorney represented a client in a personal injury action. The client had collected workermen's compensation benefits from the insurance company and that company was entitled to a lien in the amount of the benefits paid against any recovery in the personal injury action. The personal injury matter settled and a check was issued, payable to the attorney, client, and insurance company. The attorney obtained the endorsements of the client and the insurance company but did not disperse any funds to the insurance company. The attorney was suspended from practice for three months for this and other acts. Concerning the issue of the failure to honor the lien, the court stated:

> "When an attorney receives money on behalf of a third party who is not his client, he nevertheless is a fiduciary as to such third party. Thus the funds in his possession are impressed with a trust and his conversion of such funds is a breach of the trust."

In the very recent case of Cooper v. State Bar (1987) 43 Cal.3d 1016, 1020, an attorney was disbarred for, among other things, failing to honor a medical lien:

> "In August 1979 Ms. M.L.M. retained petitioner to represent her in a personal injury action. A $3,500 settlement was paid to petitioner, who then failed to pay his client's outstanding medical bill in the amount of $1,116 to the Jacobs Medical Group, although both the client and petitioner had signed a medical lien. The review department concluded that in this matter petitioner had wilfully failed to perform the legal services for which he had been employed and had wilfully misappropriated the $1,116 for his own use."

I have enclosed a copy of the full text of both opinions for your information.

Since the failure of an attorney to honor a valid lien is already considered unethical and therefore serves as a basis for the imposition of attorney discipline, I can only suggest that you encourage members of the California Chiropractic Association to file a complaint with the State Bar if this unfortunate conduct occurs. Any such complaints should be directed to:

Office of Investigations
State Bar of California
1230 West Third Street
Los Angeles, CA 90017
(800) 843-9053

As to an attorney levying "administrative charges" against the payment to the doctors, such conduct, absent an agreement to levy such charges, considered in the totality of the circumstances, might well serve as the basis for imposition of discipline.

In addition, I have forwarded your letter and enclosures to the Committee on Professional Responsibility and Conduct and have requested them to consider issuing an advisory ethics opinion on this topic to raise the level of consciousness of the members of the bar concerning this problem.

I hope the foregoing addresses your concerns. Should you have any additional comments or questions, please do not hesitate to contact me.

Very truly yours,

P. Terry Anderlini
President, State Bar
of California

THE STATE BAR OF CALIFORNIA
845 SOUTH FIGUEROA STREET LOS ANGELES, CALIFORNIA 90017-2515

OFFICE OF CHIEF TRIAL COUNSEL
INTAKE

TELEPHONE: (213) 765-1000
FAX: (213) 765-1168
http://www.calbar.ca.gov

Dear Sir or Madam:

In order to help us evaluate and process your complaint, please complete the California Attorney Complaint Form. The Attorney Complaint Form is available in the "Quick Links" section of the State Bar's website at www.calbar.ca.gov or by going to http://calbar.ca.gov/Attorneys/LawyerRegulation.aspx. You may fill out the Attorney Complaint Form online prior to printing and mailing it to the State Bar's Intake Department. (If you can't fill out the form online, download and print it before filling it out by hand.)

You may also use the State Bar's "Attorney Search" tool to see whether the attorney has a public record of prior discipline in California and whether the attorney is licensed to practice law in California. To find an attorney, go to www.calbar.ca.gov and type the attorney's name in the box. You can also go to http://members.calbar.ca.gov/fal/MemberSearch/QuickSearch.

- Please provide your name, address, zip code, email address (if available), and telephone numbers (work, home and cell).
- Be sure to give the full name, address and phone number of the attorney you are complaining about. If you wish to complain about more than one attorney, use a separate form for each attorney.
- If any of the blank spaces do not apply to your case, write N/A (Not Applicable). If you do not know the size of the attorney's law firm, please state "Unknown" in response to item (7).
- Date and sign the form.
- On a separate sheet of paper, tell us about your complaint against the attorney. Tell us what the attorney did or failed to do that you believe may warrant disciplinary action. We need to know the background of your case. Tell us in your own words what happened.
    - If your complaint is about the attorney you hired, tell us: When did you hire the attorney? What agreement did you make with the attorney? Was the agreement verbal or in writing?
    - If the complaint is about an attorney who has not represented you, please tell us: What is the connection you have with this attorney? If the attorney is representing a person or entity in a dispute with you, please identify that person or entity and explain the nature of the dispute.
- Provide any helpful documents. Send only copies and keep the originals. All documents you send, originals or copies, become the property of the State Bar and are subject to future destruction.
    - If you are complaining about an attorney who represented you, provide copies of written fee agreements, payments or other letters (written or electronic) to the attorney. It may be helpful to provide copies of the front and back sides of all canceled checks and/or copies of receipts showing your payments to the attorney. Any documents in your possession could be very helpful.
    - If you are complaining about some other attorney, provide any court documents or correspondence with the attorney which will help to explain your complaint. If you are represented by counsel in the matter involving the

attorney, please provide your attorney's name, address and telephone number.

If you are not fluent in English and need translation services in order to communicate with the State Bar, please tell us on the complaint form in the section entitled "Translation Information." Please be aware that providing formal translation may delay our communications with you. If you have someone who can provide your own translation assistance and will agree to accept communications from the State Bar in English, please let us know in response to item (8) on the complaint form.

The State Bar will review and evaluate your complaint to determine whether investigation and prosecution is appropriate. You will be notified of our decision in writing. Thank you for your cooperation.

The State Bar of California, Office of Chief Trial Counsel

Some Things You Should Know

The Office of Chief Trial Counsel (OCTC) reviews complaints of unethical conduct by attorneys licensed to practice in California. Should OCTC prosecute allegations contained in your complaint, you may be required to testify before the State Bar Court in order to prove charges against the attorney(s) involved. Below is a list of what OCTC can and cannot do when it considers a complaint against an attorney:

- OCTC can recommend that an attorney be disciplined only for a violation of the California State Bar Act or the California Rules of Professional Conduct.
- OCTC cannot act as your attorney or otherwise help you in legal matters connected with your complaint. For example, OCTC cannot give you legal advice or perform legal service for you (such as pursuing damages or other legal action against the attorney(s) involved in your complaint). You may have legal remedies available to you, but OCTC cannot advise you on your rights in a given situation or what you should do. The State Bar is not a court that can provide civil remedies to you.
- OCTC cannot give you the name of a particular attorney to help you with your legal matters. The State Bar does certify lawyer referral services, and a list of certified lawyer referral services is available on the State Bar's website at http://www.calbar.ca.gov or by calling (800) 843-9053. Also, the State Bar pamphlet "How Can I Find & Hire the Right Lawyer?" is available on the State Bar's website by searching for "Consumer Pamphlets."
- OCTC can seek discipline for an attorney's failure to refund an unearned fee or failure to account for fees. Please keep in mind, however, that attorney fees are not refundable simply because you are dissatisfied with your attorney's services. In other words, OCTC cannot decide whether an attorney's fee is reasonable. If you are disputing your attorney's fees, you may seek to resolve the dispute through a fee arbitration process. Information about fee arbitration is available from the State Bar's website at http://www.calbar.ca.gov or by calling (800) 843-9053.
- OCTC can seek an order of restitution if an attorney has misappropriated client funds. In addition, the State Bar's Client Security Fund (CSF) may reimburse funds dishonestly taken by the attorney (but not simply because the lawyer acted incompetently, committed malpractice or failed to take certain action). CSF cannot process applications for reimbursement until final discipline has been ordered against the attorney by the California Supreme Court. An application for reimbursement from CSF is available from the State Bar's website at http://www.calbar.ca.gov or by calling (800) 843-9053.
- If you have further questions, you may call the Intake Unit's complaint line at (800) 843-9053. Also, the State Bar pamphlet "Having A Problem With Your Lawyer" is available on the State Bar's web site by searching for Consumer Pamphlets. The pamphlet has helpful answers to questions about dealing with an attorney.

THE STATE BAR OF CALIFORNIA
CALIFORNIA ATTORNEY COMPLAINT FORM

Read instructions before filling in this form.

Please mail to: Office of Chief Trial Counsel / Intake Dept., State Bar of California
845 South Figueroa Street, Los Angeles, California 90017-2515

(1) Your contact information:

Your name: ______________________

Your address: ______________________

Your city, state & zip code: ______________________

Your email address: ______________________

Your telephone numbers:

Home ____________ *Work* ____________ *Cell* ____________

(2) **Attorney's contact information:** Please provide the name, address and telephone number of the attorney(s) you are complaining about. (NOTE: If you are complaining about more than one attorney, please use a separate form or include on a separate sheet for each attorney the information requested in items #2 through #7.)

Attorney's name: ______________________

Attorney's address: ______________________

Attorney's city, state & zip code: ______________________

Attorney's telephone number: ______________________

Attorney's California bar license number: ______________________

(3) Have you or a member of your family complained to the State Bar about this attorney previously?

Yes ☐ No ☐

(4) Did you employ the attorney? Yes ☐ No ☐

If "Yes," give the approximate date you employed the attorney and the amount, if any, paid to the attorney.

Date employed: ____________ Amount paid (if any): $ ____________

If "No," what is your connection with the attorney(s)? Explain briefly.

____

____

____

____

(5) Include with this form (on a separate piece of paper) a statement of what the attorney(s) did or did not do that is the basis of your complaint. Please state the facts as you understand them. Do not include opinions or arguments. If you employed the attorney(s), state what you employed the attorney(s) to do. Sign and date each separate piece of paper. Additional information may be requested. (Attach copies of pertinent documents such as a copy of the fee agreement, cancelled checks or receipts, and relevant correspondence.)

(6) If your complaint is about a lawsuit, answer the following, if known:

a. Name of court (For example, Superior Court and name of the county)

____

b. Title of the suit (For example, Smith v. Jones)

____

c. Case number of the suit ____________________

d. Approximate date the suit was filed ____________________

e. If you are not a party to this suit, what is your connection with it? Explain briefly.

____
____
____

(7) Size of law firm complained about:

☐ 1 Attorney
☐ 2 – 10 Attorneys
☐ 11 + Attorneys
☐ Government Attorney
☐ Unknown

(8) Translation Information:

If you require that the State Bar utilize formal translation services in order to process your complaint, it may delay our communications with you. Is someone available to provide translation assistance for you so that the State Bar may communicate with you in English?

Yes ☐ No ☐

If "no," state the language in which you need formal translation:

____

Signature____________________ Date: ____________________

Appendix C: MedPay Collection Kit

SHAWNSTEEL
LAW FIRM

MED PAY COLLECTION KIT

Three Easy Steps:

1. **Demand Letter:**

   Send a 'demand' letter on your stationary with a deadline. See attached. It s especially important to have your patient co-sign the letter. This educates patients ard motivates them. It also sends a powerful message to the 1st Party Med Pay Carrier that their own insured is making a personal demand on them not merely the doctor.

2. **Department of Insurance [DOI] Complaint:**

   The day following the Demand letter's deadline, complete the DOI form and have the patient sign the complaint. The patient will be further engaged with payment of their own bill.

   The insurance companies do not welcome complaints from the DOI. Be sure to send copies of the complaint to the adjuster and their supervisor.

3. **Small Claims Lawsuit:**

   California's generous small claims jurisdiction permits suits up to $10,000 if you are an individual or a sole proprietor. Corporations and other entities are limited to $5,000. In addition, a party (individuals or corporations) can file no more than two claims exceeding $2,500 in any court throughout the State of California during a calendar year.

   But, once again, you need to have your patient agree to serve as a co-plaintiff against their own insurance company. You can't sue by yourself with only an Assignment of Benefits.

   The insurance company cannot bring their attorneys. The claims manager and the adjuster can represent the insurance company if you name them as defendants.

   If your patient does not care to cooperate, then they immediately qualify to pay the difference owed by their own insurance company to you.

JohnTawlian@shawnsteel.com | (800) 626-0003

Beverly Brighter, DC
Chiropractic Clinic
143 Arizona Street, Malibu, CA 90542
Office: 310-777-1234 | Fax: 310-777-1235
Email: bbchirodc@nomail.com

Today's Date

Via Certified Mail

Insurance Company
Address 1
Address 2
Attn: Adjuster, Claim no. ##

RE: DEMAND FOR MED PAY PAYMENT; DUE IN 7 DAYS BY 5 PM

Our Patient	**: Lisa Anyman**
Your Insured	**: Daniel Anyman**
Your Claim No.	**: 123-456-AB**
Date Accident	**: 02-01-2019**

Dear Mr./Ms. Adjuster:

On behalf of our patient, *LISA ANYMAN*, we demand that *INSURANCE COMPANY* make immediate payment of the legitimate fees charged to our patient, your insured. We are sure that you are familiar with the Insurance Code Section 790.03 which requires *INSURANCE COMPANY*'s good faith when dealing with its own insured.

Unfortunately, *INSURANCE COMPANY* has failed to provide appropriate protection in order to pay fair and proper medical fees. *INSURANCE COMPANY*'s last letter reducing payment is without excuse or justification. Therefore, we inform you that, along with our patient, we will be forced to file a formal complaint against *INSURANCE COMPANY* within seven [7] days from the date of this letter to the Department of Insurance [DOI].

In addition, we will be forced to file suit against *INSURANCE COMPANY* for full tender of our legitimate and reasonable medical fees.

We prefer not to take these measures. But *INSURANCE COMPANY*'s unilateral action leaves us and our patient without any further choices. We trust *INSURANCE COMPANY* will take the reasonable approach and pay the rest of the benefits due to our patient, your insured.

Sincerely,

Dr. Beverly Brighter **Lisa Anyman: Patient and Insured**

APPENDIX D: REQUEST FOR ASSISTANCE (RFA)

STATE OF CALIFORNIA — Ricardo Lara, *Insurance Commissioner*

DEPARTMENT OF INSURANCE
CONSUMER SERVICES AND MARKET CONDUCT BRANCH
CONSUMER SERVICES DIVISION
300 SOUTH SPRING STREET, SOUTH TOWER
LOS ANGELES, CA 90013
www.insurance.ca.gov
CSD-001-P
Revised: 01/07/2019

REQUEST FOR ASSISTANCE (RFA)

Name________________________ Daytime Phone: ( ) __________

Address ________________________ Alternate Phone: ( ) __________

City /Zip ________________________ Email address: __________

Name of the policyholder if different from your name:

Type of Insurance: Auto ☐ Home ☐ Life/Annuity ☐ Long-Term Care ☐ Other ☐ ______

Complete name of insurance company involved: ______________

Policy number: __________ Claim number: __________

Date loss occurred or began (if applicable):

Insurance Broker/Agent (if applicable): __________ Broker/Agent License Number: ______

Broker/Agent Phone Number: __________ *Broker/Agent Email Address:* __________

Broker/Agent Street Address: __________ *City/State:* ______/____ *Zip:* ______

Have you contacted the company, agent or broker? Yes ☐ No ☐

If yes, state the date(s) and person(s) contacted:

Have you reported this to any other governmental agency? Yes ☐ No ☐

Name of Agency: ______________________

Date Reported: *Case Number*

Have you previously written to the Department of Insurance about this matter? Yes ☐ No ☐
File number (if available) ____________________ *Date* ____________________

Are you represented by an attorney in this matter? Yes ☐ No ☐

Has a lawsuit been filed? Yes ☐ No ☐

Is the case currently in active litigation? Yes ☐ No ☐ *If yes, we will defer the regulatory investigation until the finality of the litigation. We ask that you still complete this form so we have a record of your issue. Once the matter is concluded, we would welcome any information regarding violations of insurance law by the insurer that you or your attorney are willing to provide.*

Briefly, describe your problem (use additional paper if needed):

____

____

____

____

____

What do you consider to be a fair resolution to your problem?

____

____

____

____

____

In order for us to effectively begin our investigation, please provide any supporting documentation you may have related to this matter along with your *Request for Assistance (RFA)*.

☐ Supporting documentation (i.e. copies of correspondence between you and the insurance company/broker-agent; declaration page of your insurance policy; canceled checks; letters of claim denial, etc.)
☐ If you wish to give authority to someone to assist you in filing this *Request for Assistance (RFA)*, please complete the *Authorization and Designation of Agent* form.

PLEASE READ:
I understand that a copy of this form and all documentation submitted will be provided to the licensee involved in this Request for Assistance.

______________________________ ______________________________
(Signature) (Date)

State of California
Department of Insurance
Authorization and Designation of Agent

- If you want to give someone the authority to assist you in the filing of your complaint please fill in Parts A and B below.
- If you are a parent or legal guardian filing this complaint for a child under the age of 18, you do not need to complete this form.
- If you are filing a complaint for a consumer who cannot complete this form and you have legal authority to act for this consumer, please complete Part B only. Also send a copy of the power of attorney for health care decisions or other legal document that says you can make decisions for the consumer.

PART A: COMPLAINANT

I allow the person named below in Part B to assist me in completing a complaint filed with the California Department of Insurance (CDI). I allow the CDI to share my personal information with the person named below in Part B. This may include information about my medical condition(s) and care if applicable and may include mental health treatment, HIV treatment or testing, alcohol or drug treatment, or other health care information.

I understand that only information related to my complaint will be shared.

My approval of this assistance is voluntary and I have the right to end it. If I want it to end, I must do so in writing.

Name of Complainant (Print) ____

Complainant Signature______________________________ Date_____________

PART B: PERSON ASSISTING THE COMPLAINANT

If Applicable, Name of Organization (Please print)

____

Name of Person Assisting (Please print)

____

Signature of Person Assisting

Address ____

Relationship to Complainant

____

Daytime Phone # ______________________ Email Address ______________________

☐ My Power of Attorney for health care decisions or other legal document is attached.

Return the completed form to California Department of Insurance, Consumer Services Division, 300 S. Spring Street, Los Angeles, CA 90013. If you have any questions, the Department can be reached at (800) 927-4357.

STATE OF CALIFORNIA — Ricardo Lara, Insurance Commissioner

DEPARTMENT OF INSURANCE

Privacy Notice on Information Collection

Request for Assistance Forms

*** This notice is provided pursuant to the Information Practices Act of 1977 (California Civil Code Section 1798.17) ***

Collection and Use of Personal Information

California Insurance Code Sections 12921 and 12921.1, and related statutes and regulations, give the California Department of Insurance (CDI) and the Consumer Services Division the authority to regulate and investigate consumer complaints. The CDI uses your information to address complaints brought to the Department's attention. Information is collected subject to limitations contained in the Information Practices Act of 1977, SAM 5300, et seq., SIMM 5305, et seq., and other applicable state and federal laws.

Providing Personal Information Is Voluntary

You do not have to provide the personal information requested. However, if you do not wish to provide us the necessary information, we may not be able to investigate your complaint. When providing information or documents, please do not include unrequested personal information, such as Social Security Numbers, Driver's License Numbers, unnecessary health-related information, and credit card or financial information.

Information Provided to CDI Is Confidential

All information you provide to us during the investigation of your complaint will be treated as a confidential communication under California Insurance Code Section 12919. We will not disclose any information to any person outside CDI, unless otherwise permitted or required by law.

Possible Disclosure of Personal Information

We may share your personal information with the insurance licensee and in the case of an Independent Medical Review with the Independent Medical Review Organization. We may also share your information with other government or regulatory agencies as permitted or required by law, or pursuant to Memorandum of Understanding.

Access to Your Information

You have the right to access records containing your personal information which are maintained by CDI. To request access, contact: CDI Privacy Officer, Legal Division, Government Law Bureau, 300 Capitol Mall, Suite 1700, Sacramento, CA 95814, (916) 492-3500.

Department Privacy Policy

The California Department of Insurance has developed policies regarding the privacy of your information. They may be viewed at www.insurance.ca.gov/privacy-policy.

INDEX

About the Authors

Shawn Steel, Esq.

Shawn Steel has chiropractic embedded in his roots. He is a member of a family that includes three generations of chiropractors (his mother, his great aunt, and his older cousin). In addition to coming from a chiropractic family, he was raised in Rock Island, Illinois, just across the Mississippi from Palmer Chiropractic College.

As an adult, he received a Secondary Standard Teaching Credential from California State University

Northridge and a Bachelor of Arts in History from the University of Southern California before going to law school and becoming the first lawyer in his family. He used his familiarity and background with chiropractic practice to forge his own path forward in law, practicing in a new field he refers to as "chiropractic law." This field focuses on training chiropractors to apply their skillsets to the legal field to serve in various capacities, including as consultants and expert witnesses in personal injury and worker's compensation cases.

As one of the primary practitioners of chiropractic law, he has lectured extensively on the subject, and has had the great honor of teaching at all three of the major chiropractic colleges in California. His pedagogy and his practice both focus on the ethics of jurisprudence as it applies to medical analysis, as well as trial strategy and specific personal injury and insurance considerations.

Alexander C. Eisner, Esq.

Alex is a trial attorney at Shawn Steel Law Firm and the head of the litigation department. He serves communities all throughout California. He also has a background in handling wrongful terminations, contract disputes, business litigation cases, and medical malpractice defense cases at the district and federal levels.

Prior to joining Shawn Steel, he was a litigator at a small, general civil litigation firm in Long Beach, California, where he ran the litigation department from 2015 to 2017, and prior to that he handled medical malpractice defense cases for Bonne, Bridges, Muller, O'Keefe, and Nichols.

Alex found his home at Shawn Steel after responding to an ad Shawn wrote titled, "Looking for Litigation Attorney for Life-Changing Opportunity." Alex was immediately tasked with learning to speak what Shawn calls "chiropractese," so he went on a chiropractic pilgrimage, visiting over fifty chiropractic offices in his first year from Humboldt County to San Diego County. Alex and Shawn became fast friends and have thoroughly enjoyed developing their tag-team style of lecturing, which keeps docs coming back year after year to hear their views on such riveting topics as ethics, jurisprudence, and common mistakes that keep Doctors of Chiropractic from getting paid.